CREATIVE ACTIVITIES
RESOURCE BOOK

CREATIVE ACTIVITIES
RESOURCE BOOK
for
Elementary School
Teachers

THOMAS N. TURNER
University of Tennessee

Reston Publishing Company
A Prentice-Hall Company
Reston, Virginia

Library of Congress Cataloging in Publication Data

Turner, Thomas N
   Creative activities resource book for elementary
school teachers.

   Bibliography: p.
   1. Creative thinking (Education)   2. Language arts
(Elementary)   3. Drama in education.   4. Activity
programs in education.   I.   Title.
LB1062.T87   372.6   78-48
ISBN 0-87909-205-X

© 1978 by Reston Publishing Company, Inc.
A Prentice-Hall Company
Reston, Virginia 22090

10 9 8 7 6 5 4 3 2 1

Printed in the United States of America

To creative teachers everywhere;
but especially to my wife, Fran,
without whose patience, constructive
suggestions, and typing skills this
book would not have been possible;
to Don Hardy, who discovered
Creative Activities in the rough; and
to Dr. John D. MacAulay—my mentor,
professional model, and friend.

Contents

Preface

This is an *unleashing* book: its primary purpose is to help teachers and children set creativity free. It contains practical (but not "canned") sets of activities. Both teachers and children will have to do some preparation and background development for most of the activities presented here, but the format includes objectives, procedures, materials, and variations that should make for easy understanding and implementation of the activities by teachers.

There are separate chapters that deal with (1) exploring the creative impulse; (2) limbering up teachers; (3) creative writing: (4) oral expression; (5) creative movement; (6) manipulatory activities; (7) thinking experiences; and (8) short-time activities.

Creative Activities Resource Book for Elementary School Teachers may be used in workshops and in-service programs as well as by the individual teacher who is seeking an activity source. I am excited and enthusiastic about its potential for creative teachers and children.

ACKNOWLEDGEMENTS

I want to thank all of the many creative teachers and students who helped with suggestions, ideas, and reactions. The original creativity class at the University of Tennessee helped build the nucleus from which this book emerged and deserves special recognition. Thanks to them all: Diana Abernathy, Patricia Rector, Donna H. Olmstead, Kristen Rogers, Betty J. Smith, William R. Livesay, Mary S. Emery, Randall K. Bassett, Penny S. Crook, Linda Parris, Elizabeth J. Brown, Victoria Kryah, James E. Comption, and Gwendolyn W. McCoig.

THOMAS N. TURNER

The Creative Impulse: Back to More than Basics

vides a variety of activities and rich experiences quite disproportionate to the exigencies of time. In a sense, it is a classroom that surrounds the child with "mind catalysts." It belies the sterile, boring, and popular stereotype. The basic principle is that creation and imagination are self-perpetuating. Once "seeded," they spread. They are productive instead of destructive, and ought to be freed, not constrained.

3. **Creative "set"**—Ordinarily, schools encourage a retentive "set." That is, they invite memory response and predictable expression. This is not undesirable, unless it impedes creative thinking. On the other hand, the creative classroom encourages a creative set, or orientation toward non-memory and unpredictable response. Usually a creative set involves a new direction in thinking or a new awareness of variable patterns of thought. Flexibility in shifting from retentive to creative thinking sets and back again when the question and situation demand is crucial in the creative classroom. One of the skills needed is the ability to identify when creative thinking is appropriate and when retentive thinking is appropriate. One approach to developing this flexibility of set is to allow a warm-up period for creative thinking—a brief "reorienting" time. Warm-up techniques include activities like asking children to make several associations from the same list of words, having children draw and label several pictures from a series of incomplete sample line drawings (geometric shapes, dots, etc.), having them list multiple uses for a series of objects, or having each child respond with a different association for a single stimulus.

A creative classroom cannot be rigidly described. Neither can a creative teacher be adequately characterized. But the quest goes on for that invaluable combination. The creative teacher and the creative classroom are the most needed things in American education. As J. D. McAulay (1974) asserts:

> In the remote past, the creative teacher believed himself to be inspired by some force external to himself (in classical times, a muse). Contemporary experience mirrors this point of view by the conviction that at the creative moment the teacher is lifted out of himself. He feels he is being taken over by the dynamics of instruction. But powerful teaching occurs when the surrendering of self to this creative power is combined with the humility of a skilled craftsman. Then the teacher is aware that creative teaching like love implies the existence of other persons if it is to have any meaning at all.[5]

CONCLUSION: CREATIVITY AND CLASSROOM DISCIPLINE

The creative impulse is present in children and teachers. To frustrate it is to contain or destroy the most productive resource in the world. Controls are needed for any society to exist, and certainly good discipline is necessary for a school. Even creativity must be controlled. But educators must not forget that the goal of discipline is self-discipline, and that the end of both is not to control freedom but rather to assure a society where individual freedom is protected. Good discipline should not imprison the creativity of the child. To forget this is to make the school a dungeon of oppression and tyranny, of control for its own sake.

The remainder of this book is built upon a number of closely related assumptions. These assumptions form the goalposts through which I think we must pass if schools are to build the creative impulse into a real force in the classroom:

1. All children are creative. It is just a matter of degree.
2. All children need to become more creative. It is a matter of their well-being and mental health.
3. Creativity can be learned, or (worse) it can be conditioned out of a child by repeated negative reinforcement or no reinforcement at all.
4. The elementary classroom can and should be a place where children learn to be more creative.
5. Teachers should themselves be creative people able to meet and assess the varied human needs and learning needs of their students.
6. *Every* classroom can be a more creatively inspiring place.
7. Creativity should receive high priority status in classroom time.
8. Life in modern American society demands more creativity to meet variety, change, and living problems than any society in the history of the world.
9. Children naturally want to be creative.
10. A stimulus-rich environment and a variety of opportunities to be original are essential for a classroom which promotes creative growth.

REFERENCES

McAulay, J. D. "A Personal View." *The Pennsylvania State University College of Education Faculty Forum.* February 5, 1974.

Parnes, S. J. *Creative Behavior Guidebook.* New York: Charles Scribner's Sons, 1967.

Smith, J. A. *Setting Conditions for Creative Teaching.* Boston: Allyn and Bacon, 1966.

Torrance, E. P. "The Creative Personality and the Ideal Pupil." *Teachers College Record.* 1963, 65, 220–226.

Yamamoto, K. *Experimental Scoring Manuals for Minnesota Tests of Creative Thinking and Writing.* Kent, Ohio: Kent State Univeristy Bureau of Educational Research, 1964.

Teacher Creativity

I often ask groups to do brief creative exercises involving music, art, or writing. A comment I often hear from teachers and students is "I'm not very creative." For the sake of courtesy I bite my tongue and clench my jaws to keep from saying—"You don't belong in teaching if you aren't" I don't want to hurt their feelings. What I really mean is that teaching demands creativity. If teachers cannot solve a hundred different problems in just as many different ways they are not going to be effective. Usually the statement "I'm not very creative" is being used as an excuse. Those who say it do not want to be judged for not doing something or not doing it well. They want to avoid being compared to others. They do not want to risk trying. The tragedy this embodies is that creativity can be enchained or diminished through disuse and negative reinforcement. As with driving a car, sewing, reading, or other skills, some people can develop higher creative thinking and action skills than others. These people become the professionals in their art. But the people who say "I'm not very creative" are admitting that they stopped risking themselves long ago because they didn't receive rewarding feedback.

The teachers who say "I'm not creative" particularly concern me because they are the professionals in a field that I believe should demand and challenge the highest levels of creative thinking. In the first place, in spite of some research evidence to the contrary, I think that for classrooms to be places where children are stimulated to their creative best, the teachers must be creative. In the second place, I think that effective teaching itself demands the utmost in personal flexibility, adaptability to complexity and change, and problem-solving skill. Teachers must respond to the learning needs, failures, frustrations and successes of children with a pulse-taking, diagnosing fluidness. They must be open to varied options. To have a "set" pattern of response is to fail with all but a few problems of teaching.

The activities in this chapter are specifically aimed at helping teachers improve their own creative skills, to "bud" and "flower" as creative individuals. Hopefully, teachers will gain in ability and insight and become more sensitive to creative children, creative ideas from children, and creative opportunities for children.

The first part of the chapter provides some limbering up exercises to help teachers free their minds. Some of these techniques can also be used with children. The second part of the chapter provides some "starters" to help the teacher in the continuous process of adapting materials and activities from textbooks and other resources. As every teacher knows, some idealized resource materials must be fitted to the needs and abilities of a particular child or group of children.

LIMBERING UP

Good athletes warm up. They go through a whole series of exercises that loosen and stimulate their muscles. They tone themselves to move smoothly and effortlessly. They sharpen their reflexes. They intensify their concentration and "oneness" with the activity at hand.

Creative thinking and expression require warm-up too. This warm-up serves many of the same purposes as an athlete's routine. It develops a "set" purposefulness in thinking that is more open to varied options, better disciplined to seek imaginative solutions through multiple alternatives.

ASSOCIATIONS

Objective: **To build power in thinking of multiple solutions to problems.**

Materials: A handwritten list of friends, classmembers, fellow teachers, or famous individuals.

Procedure: Move down the list, trying to associate three objects with each of the names. These can be things you see the person with regularly or objects you merely associate with their character. Now switch to abstract ideas like colors or character traits and try to think of three associations for each individual.

Variation: Try thinking of three questions you would like to ask the individual but will not, or three things you would like to tell them but will not.

MY COMMUNICATION

Objective: **To develop a more accurate perception of how time is spent.**

Procedure: Think about the way you spend your time from 8:00 AM until 8:00 PM.
   A. Write down an estimate of the amount of time you spend in communication; speaking, listening, reading, writing.
   B. The next day try to keep a record based on 15-minute intervals, and fill in the following table:

	Speaking	Listening	Writing	Reading	Other	Remarks
8:00						
8:15						
etc.						

Conversation may be divided between speaking and listening. Be your own judge in making the division. You may want to include talking to yourself.
   C. After recording your communication for the day, look at the percentages of time spent in each form of communication.
   D. Compare your record with estimates for the average American's communication time. If the entire 12 hours were spent in communication this would mean about 5 hours listening, 4 hours speaking, 2 hours reading, 1 hour writing.

   Listening—42 percent   Reading—15 percent
   Speaking—32 percent   Writing—11 percent

   E. Make a list of the obvious conclusions about your personal communication.
   F. Decide what changes you would like to see in your patterns of time use.

Variation: Take a shorter block of time, say an hour, in which you are purposefully engaged mostly in one form of communication. Make a pencil mark for each time you are distracted.

VISUAL SYMMETRY: WORDS

Objective: **To develop appreciation for and sensitivity to the sensory power of language.**

Procedure: Give words visual form by arranging as many repetitions of each letter as necessary to form a symmetrical shape. Let the sound of the letter and the meaning of the word suggest its visualization.

Examples: "Why?" may become
In "what" the "w" and "h" may take a more closed form in your mind.
The unity and symmetry of the letter shapes prevent spelling confusion even in double letter words like "running."

Variation: Try adjusting the size and style of letters, fitting letters within letters (   ) for example.

VISUAL SYMMETRY: LANGUAGE

Objective: **To develop visual images from sentences or phrases.**

Procedure: Try building short one- or two-line poems repeating words to produce visual symmetrical images; interlock the words with common letters.

Example: "A great gray goblin"

```
            YARGRAY
               R
               E
               A
               T
            AAA E
               E
               R
         NILBOGOBLIN
```

Variation: Arrange poetic lines into visual forms such as plane geometric shapes (circles, trapezoids, parallelograms), spokes from a common wheel hub, or waves.

WORD CHAINS

Objective: **To increase powers of association and reduce the tendency to dead-end on first ideas.**

Procedure: From a single word or idea form a series of associations. Use each new word associated as a "trigger" to the next. Thus by the time you stop (there is never an end to the possibilities) the end word may seem unrelated to the first. Work within a specified time limit (60 seconds, or 3 minutes).

Example: Dog— leash— chain— slavery— freedom— democracy— America— justice— court— judge— jury— deliberation— decision— religion

Variations: 1. Relate all the associations to the original word to see how many different ideas can be generated.

   Example: dog— cat— leash— hair— bark— growl— friend— bite— point— Lassie— hunting— protection— puppy

   2. Make chains of created words using compounds and inflectional endings. Invent imaginative meanings.

   Example: invent— devent— intervent— inventoress— invensionette— invenience— coninvension— revent

LIFE LINE

Objective: **To help review and clarify significant events in personal experience.**

Procedure: Diagram your life to the present and project your expectations of the future. Develop your own symbols as you like. Vary the curve and shape of the line to represent the happiness, tumultuousness, sadness, or tedium of the event.

Variation: Project a fantasy life line into the future.

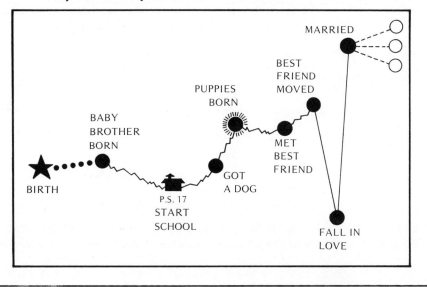

PUZZLING IT OUT

Objective: **To become more aware of the learning value of jigsaw activities.**

Materials: Several commercial jigsaw puzzles and puzzle games such as Soma Cube, Hi-Q, Pythagoras.

Procedure: Spend enough time working with each puzzle to understand what makes it difficult and intriguing. (This may not require that you take time to completely solve the puzzle, but you may feel compelled to.) Now try to draw your own puzzle by beginning with a shapeless closed curve. Divide the figure into several pieces to make the puzzle. It may be judged "good" (that is, challenging) if some pieces fit together in several ways.

Variation: Make puzzles using regular plane geometric shapes (triangles, squares, rectangles) comprised of other geometric figures. Use magazine pictures for the puzzles so that clues to successful completion can be seen in the pictures that emerge.

TEACHING REVIEW

Objective: **To use teaching time more effectively.**

Procedure: Take a one-hour period (a good hour or a bad one) out of the last school day. Review how you spent it (what you taught, what you said, what children said to you). Reconstruct the time as carefully as possible in your mind. After this review list five things you would do differently and five things you would do the same if you could relive that hour.

Variations:
1. Make a list of five things said and a better way to say each.
2. Make a list of prescriptions for problems encountered during the time reviewed.

CHILD TYPING

Objective: **To clarify perceptions of the distinctive individuality of each child.**

Materials: A list of all the children you teach.

Procedure: Write an adjective next to each child's name which describes his or her character. Try to select a positive and unique descriptive adjective for each child. Reexamine your list and make a second effort, but this time try to characterize your own relationship with the child. (Again use a different word for each child.)

Variation: Try selecting adjectives that reflect the best aspects of your relationships with the children and your perception of them.

ROOM CHANGE

Objective: **To eliminate the distraction of idealizing about teaching improvements.**

Procedure: Imagine yourself with unlimited funds for improving instruction in your classroom. Write down all the physical changes (at least ten) you would make to your teaching space to make it a better learning atmosphere. List specific types of classroom materials that you would purchase. List or record on a cassette the differences these changes would make in your effectiveness as a teacher. Go back and look at the existing facilities. This time list three changes that are most crucial and make these your priorities. Make another list of small- or no-cost items that would enhance the classroom atmosphere. Make a list of things that should be eliminated.

Variation: Repeat the same procedure, but this time list things you have already acquired. Be thankful—if only for your ability to scrounge.

DAY-STRETCHER

Objective: **To increase the teacher's ability to meet the individual needs of children.**

Procedure: List the items in the school day for which you need more time (more time to give your students personal attention and/or more time for the children to learn). Be specific—(for example, don't just list more time to give special individual attention but "more time to give Johnny Smith help with his spelling"). Rank these items according to importance (give items of equal importance the same rank). When this is completed, try to make a list of time-wasting things you do and time spent on less important tasks. Finally, resolve that for one school day you will give the time needed for your highest priority items on the first list.

Variation: Write the high priority items on one side of the blackboard and the time-wasters on the other. Have children keep score of your success in devoting attention to high priority items and in reducing time-wasting efforts.

DEVELOPING A NEW SET TOWARD THE PROBLEM CHILD

Objective: **To find new approaches to difficult teaching situations.**

Material: A casette recorder

Procedure: Identify the child in your class who troubles you most, causes you the greatest frustration. The child may be a discipline problem, have learning or attention difficulties, or have health, attendance or home problems. Allow yourself to focus exclusively on this child for a few minutes. Using the recorder, try to clarify and describe as exactly as possible the things that bother you. Next examine the reasons for your frustration by trying to identify the child's weaknesses and your own self-doubts. Finally, try to think of each of the things you have done to meet this frustrating situation. After a few days, replay the recording. List ten things you are not doing that might be tried. If you believe you have exhausted all the realistic possibilities, attempt to generate some humorous, ridiculous, and fantastic ideas. Even if this is impossible, just the effort may lead you in new directions.

Variations
1. Do the same thing in isolating a problem that involves several children.
2. Try to identify the child with a familiar character in a story. Think about the psychology of the fictional character and the kinds of approaches or gestures that were effective in the story situation.

ADAPTATION OF RESOURCES

Creative teaching involves a persistent, scavengerlike search for the most advantageous use of resources. Sometimes materials must be adapted not only to the subject or skill being taught, but to children's special needs, interests, and levels of ability. Teachers must seek interesting new ideas that are easily modified and applicable to classroom use. Making the best of familiar resources, becoming more aware of alternative materials, and introducing new ideas result in stimulating and revitalized classroom activities.

The ideas offered in this part of the chapter serve as catalysts to teacher thinking and ideation. Although they can be classified as teaching activities or aids, their main purpose is to motivate creative effort. The teacher can use them as stimuli in planning classroom activities and in developing variations on the suggested themes. Hopefully he or she will be able to adapt them to the needs and interests of particular grades or school cultures. By simplifying or expanding these ideas the teacher will become more sensitive to his or her own creative potential and that of students as well.

The first group of ideas offered in this section is a set of story starters. These are short paragraphs that present incomplete situations or describe particular problems or dilemmas having many possible resolutions. Hopefully these highly fantasized problem situations pique the imagination, but this is not their only purpose. The main quest is to see how situations like these can be used with children to capture their most varied attention and encourage their response.

Unlike the rest of the activities in this book, these story premises have sample questions, variations, and adaptations for younger children. The word *sample* has been intentionally added as a reminder that these ideas only initiate a thinking process.

One of the purposes of story premises is to provide experience with the flexibility of solutions to various problem situations. Fantasy serves better than reality because the individual does not feel bound by the natural laws and known rules of the real world.

From the story premises the chapter moves on to free and/or available teaching materials. Teachers are invited to look at the many content-laden items and skill building tools to be found all around. The creative teacher should become an innovative scavenger.

The chapter moves finally to risk-taking experiences. Since people must decide when they will risk thinking creatively, this seemed to be an appropriate note on which to end. These exercises consist of a series of personal brainstorming tasks. They are aimed at determining what conditions are necessary before people take the risk of being creative. Hopefully these exercises will provide tools for the meaningful examination of this question.

STORY STARTERS

THE MIND READER

Objective: To better realize that what people think and what they say differ significantly.

Premise: Imagine that you suddenly acquired a mysteriously unusual power—to read other people's minds, but only at certain times: (1) when they ask a question you know the question before they ask it; (2) when they are thinking about you, you know their thoughts.

Sample Questions: What four real or imaginary people would you meet first? What words would they be likely to say? What would be the reactions of people you know if you answered before they asked the question?

Variation: You are able to read the thoughts of animals and thus communicate with them.

Adaptation for Young Children: Ask what they would discover if they could read someone's mind. Avoid complicating the question with additional conditions.

THE BIG WAR

Objective: To help develop sensitivity to the responsibilities of having power.

Premise: The earth is engaged in a global war but it is a strange war. The sides are so evenly matched that neither dares to use its terrible distructive weapons. You alone could change this. You know something that would help your own people win, but it would mean the deaths of millions, including young, innocent children. You are offered anything you want, if you will only reveal this knowledge. You are threatened with torture if you don't tell.

Sample Questions: What could this knowledge be? Who would you ask for advice?

Variations: You have knowledge that would save lives but prolong the war and make the outcome indecisive. Your side is now winning and wants you to keep silent.

Adaptation for Young Children: The war is between the elephants and the mice, not people. The children must describe some special knowledge that these animals possess.

THE DISAPPEARANCE

Objective: To expand the range of possible changes that individuals are able to imagine in themselves.

Premise: On a sunny spring day you and a friend are taking a hike in an unfamiliar woods. Suddenly the sky becomes cloudy and ominous, the woods grow quiet, and a mysterious tension pervades the atmosphere. The two of you stop and look a little apprehensively at each other. As the sky becomes increasingly dark you suddenly sense that your friend has disappeared from your side. Then you feel your arms gripped from behind by an invisible slimy-feeling force. You are unable to scream or breathe as the force stretches you until you feel you are going to burst. You slip into unconsciousness and float in darkness. Awakening, you see a single candle flickering in the distance. You do not seem the same as you were before.

Sample Questions: What happened to your friend? What changes in your body could have occurred? How is your mind different?

Variation: You read about the strange disappearance and somehow understand what has happened.

Adaptation for Young Children: Remove the fearfulness of the situation by changing the circumstances of the disappearance, perhaps substituting a magical fairyland or dream world for the dark and gloomy woods. At the very least, the child should be doing the "grabbing" in the story instead of being gripped by the mysterious force.

✦ RETURNING TO RULE

Objective: To help develop the realization that changes occur in our absence.

Premise: After a long trip to the mountains, you return to what you think is your home. But now people are bowing before you as you walk by. Everyone is worshipping you and you don't understand. They seem to think you are a returning emperor or famed ruler and although you try to explain the mistake to them, somehow they cannot understand. They continue to pay you homage.

Sample Questions: What about you gives this impression? What other changes have occurred while you were away?

Variation: All your relatives and friends act as though they do not know you, as though you were a stranger.

Adaptation for Young Children: Have the children pretend they are crowned kings or queens after returning home. Ask them to imagine their first act as ruler.

THE ACCIDENT VICTIM

Objective: To develop understanding of the difficulty of communication.

Premise: You witness an automobile accident and are the only one who goes to help. You find an injured girl who has strange speech. She is difficult to understand, that is, until you realize that she answers all your questions in an ancient language. It seems ridiculous that you can understand her at all, but it seems to grow easier each moment.

Sample Question: What do you think you should do for the girl?

Variation: The girl was magically taken from her own time by a modern magician who was killed in the accident. How can you help her return to her own age?

Adaptation for Young Children: Discuss the possible problems of communicating with someone from the past. Relate this to the problems of understanding an animal or an infant.

✦ THE SHRINKING EGG PEOPLE

Objective: To help expand the idea that differences in people do not necessarily affect the way they should be treated.

Premise: On a distant planet in the Amokianic Galaxy, the people seem like earthlings except for one peculiarity. They are all born from eggs and are at least sixteen feet tall at birth. As they age, they grow smaller instead of larger. By the time they reach maturity they are only 40 inches high.

Sample Questions: Where do the eggs come from? Why do people grow "down" instead of up.

Variation: A dozen of these eggs are delivered to earth.

Adaptation for Young Children: Ask each child what would come out of an egg 20 feet high? Discuss how they would act if they found such an egg.

HALLOWEEN PARTY

Objective: **To develop greater abilities to deal with fear-causing situations.**

Premise: At midnight on Halloween you wake up and are hungry. You start to go downstairs to get a snack when you hear a spine-tingling cackle. You look around and gasp at the sight of a skeleton, a ghost, a bearded giant, and a mummy, all dancing and performing feats of magic. Suddenly they lunge toward you.

Sample Questions: Is there a magic word or an explanation that would prevent this attack? Is there some real explanation for these apparently ghostly beings? Who could you call for help?

Variations: Treat the incident as it would be in a Saturday morning television cartoon. Add a magic ring that can be rubbed to send its wearer to another place or summon another power.

Adaptation for Young Children: Have the children describe the ten creatures they would be most frightened to encounter or most excited to meet.

STAR WISH

Objective: **To encourage goal setting and help clarify expectations.**

Premise: Every night you make a wish upon the first star you see as you lay in bed. It is fun to do and more a way of daydreaming than something you really believe. But one July night you are hot and you wish "I want it to snow!" Before the thought is out it starts snowing. You wonder at the strange coincidence but before long, you realize it is not a coincidence at all. Your wishes really are coming true, all of them. But you soon become aware of an attendant curse. Each time you wish your hair grows longer. Naturally you find a professional wizard who knows all about these magical dilemmas. The wizard tells you that if you cut your hair even a little, all your power will disappear.

Sample Questions: Would it be best to make a lot of wishes at once and then get a haircut, or to figure out a way of managing your rapidly growing locks? How did you get the power?

Variations:
1. Your hair cannot be cut. It breaks even the hardest steel scissors and knives.
2. You find you make a lot of wishes you really don't mean.
3. You pick up a stick and feel a strange, whirring sensation about it. As you mutter "I hope it doesn't rain," the "wand" wriggles and it starts raining! Then you say, "Oh, I hope my cat's inside, out of this rain," and presto, your cat is beside you, getting drenched. You then realize you have a "backwards" magic wand! What are you to do now?

Adaptation for Young Children: Give younger children a series of open-ended sentences to finish about their wishes.

Example:

I wish my mother would stop _____

I wish I could _____

I wish my friend _____ could have three things: (1) _____ (2) _____ (3) _____

I wish I could go to _____

I wish tomorrow would be _____

I wish I could run _____

I wish I could have _____

I wish my father could find _____

WORLD LAW

Objective: **To broaden understanding of the purposes of rules.**

Premise: You and any people you choose as a committee must write all the rules by which this world should operate. Choose the people, and write a set of "Ten Commandments" or laws for the world community.

Sample Questions: Should the rules be listed in order of importance? Who would serve on your committee?

Variations:
1. The rules will be obeyed in reverse (e.g., if you command people not to steal they will all steal).
2. List priorities for self-improvement.

Adaptation for Young Children: Have children formulate the rules for a good family, the rules every child ought to have to obey, or perhaps the rules for responsible pet ownership.

FROZEN STIFF

Objective: **To develop empathy and understanding for small animals in a world controlled by stronger and more powerful creatures.**

Premise: The entire world is slowly being frozen in position. You do not understand what's happening until you see a giant blue squirrel about to freeze the only other still functioning human being.

Sample Questions: How does the squirrel freeze people? How can you prevent this creature from freezing you?

Variation: You alone are frozen and your friends cannot understand it. You are conscious but cannot move or speak.

Adaptation for Young Children: Have children talk about living in a world where each animal is a different bright color.

BIG BOSS

Objective: **To develop a sense of the limitations of one's power by another's rights.**

Premise: Without any apparent reason you are elected dictator of the world for life. You have decided to plan the perfect world. Your first decision is to exile certain law offenders to an island where they must live apart from law-abiding citizens. What are the laws which will bring this punishment?

Sample Questions: Does anyone have the right to be a dictator? Do you think a dictator would ever be elected? Do you think people could agree on what makes a perfect world?

Variation: In a world ruled by such a dictator, you are the first judge (or first exiled offender).

Adaptation for Young Children: Have each child tell what he or she thinks is the perfect flower, food, etc. Then have them vote. The winning votes will make up the "perfect world." Have the children draw a world that has *only* these flowers, foods, etc.

BOMB THREAT

Objective: **To increase awareness of the constant threats to the peace and safety of society.**

Premise: You have just received a bomb in the mail! Attached is a note which states: "This is a nuclear bomb. It will go off in one hour from the time you first touch it. All within ten miles will be instantaneously killed. Everyone within a twenty-mile radius will be deformed by the effects of radioactivity." Looking at a clock you realize that you first touched the explosive eight minutes ago.

Sample Questions:

What must you do?

Who would send such a bomb?

Who would you notify?

What would you do to stop bombs from being planted in buildings or sent through the mails?

Adaptation for Young Children: Have the children send a note to someone else in the class telling them something very nice, either complimenting them or just expressing friendship. Do not have them sign the note. Then ask each child to guess who wrote the note they received. Make sure all children receive notes.

TIME MACHINE

Objective: **To better understand time concepts—that time passes slower or faster depending on how involved one is.**

Premise: A crazy inventor who is a friend of yours says he has a "time machine." You enthusiastically agree to test his invention to determine if it functions properly. Once inside you discover that your body has shrunk to microscopic size. Also, you realize that you are not going backward into time, nor forward, but you apparently are going "inside" time! Time seems to be slowed to the point where minute sequential motions are visible. You are able to see sound waves vibrating, grass growing, body cells and hair growing.

Sample Question: What does it mean to be inside of time?

Variations: You are transported to another age. You are a slow motion or time elapse camera.

Adaptation for Young Children: Have children role play events or developmental stages in their own lives. Begin with simple role assignments such as being a baby. Then progress to more specific events or more difficult parts.

ROBINSON CRUSOE OF THE TWENTY-FIFTH CENTURY

Objective: **To develop better abilities in getting along with others.**

Premise: During the Great Space and Sea War you had been a general, but now, defeated, you are a prisoner of war. Along with the other prisoners you are being transported to the enemy's home across the great sea. A storm comes up, the ship sinks, and everyone drowns except you and your most hated enemy. You both swim to an island that appears to have been quickly and recently deserted. The evidence indicates that this civilization was at least 20 years more advanced than your own. You and your enemy are alone on the island together.

Sample Question: Can you live peacefully with your enemy?

Variation: You are alone on the island.

Adaptation for Young Children: Have younger children make a model of an island using a sand table. Create a make-believe city.

A VISIT TO GNOMEWORLD

Objective: **To develop power to envision different types of worlds.**

Premise: One day you are sitting on a bench in the park. It is a happy kind of day. You hum to yourself, close your eyes and just let your mind drift. Suddenly, you are startled by a peculiar sound and opening your eyes you glimpse a small gnome leaping from a nearby tree. After talking with him for a few moments, he starts pleading with you to come with him. Since you don't seem to have a choice you follow him to the tree, into his world. As you enter you stand amazed at this new discovery.

Sample Question: What other choices would you have?

Variation: You are turned into a liquid and flow down to the roots of the tree.

Adaptation for Young Children: Have children pretend to be elves and tell you about their world.

SUSPENDED ANIMATION

Objective: **To develop an awareness of the changes that have occurred in the way people live.**

Premise: Suppose you were born in 1480 and at the age of 20 you were somehow suspended. You have slept for 500 years. Now in 1980 you awaken to a new world.

Sample Questions: What would you want to see first? What are the most important changes you would see? What would be strange to you?

Variation: You had been a conscious observer of human life even though you were unable to move. You witnessed the changes as they occurred.

Adaptation for Young Children: Have children pretend they were boys or girls when the oldest person in their family was a child. Then have them share their thoughts with the class.

PERFECT PLACES

Objective: **To clarify personal concepts of the ideal place to live.**

Materials: Short descriptive accounts from several of the major religious publications depicting an idealized afterlife.

Premise: In a vision you are able to see the biblical Garden of Eden. Then you see a vision of heaven!

Sample Questions: How are the two different? Why were you granted the visions?

Variation: List characteristics that describe your idea of a perfect heaven or hell.

Adaptation for Young Children: Have each child describe one thing he might see if he were granted similar visions. Ask each to offer one word describing heaven.

ANIMAL TRUTH

Objective: **To develop better understanding of the sources of fear.**

Materials: Pictures of various real and make-believe animals.

Premise: Pretend you have just been reborn as a full grown animal (e.g., mink, sea urchin). Describe your adjustment. Describe your first fearful experience as a reincarnated being.

Sample Questions: What advantages do animals have over humans? What do you like least?

Variations:
1. You are changed into an inanimate object.
2. You are born as a baby animal.

Adaptation for Young Children: Have the children tell about the animals or things they would most like to be. Then have them pantomime.

 INVISIBLE INVADERS

Objective: **To develop skills in problem solving as it relates to communication and persuasion.**

Premise: The earth has just been invaded by creatures from outer space. As you try to spread the news, you realize you are the only person who can see them!

Sample Questions: What will you do? How will people react to you? How will you convince them that you aren't crazy? What can invisible creatures do?

Variation: The creatures are friendly and want you to communicate to the world for them.

Adaptation for Young Children: Have children pantomime an invasion of invisible insects or mice.

THE VOICES

Objective: **To develop the ability to project many possibilities from limited information.**

Premise: While walking across a field you fall down a partially hidden, stone stairway. At the bottom you hit your head on an exposed wooden knob. Barely able to move or see in the dark, you grope to find what struck your head. Finally you locate the knob and as you grasp it, a concealed trap door seems to move. You almost lapse into total unconsciousness. You hear voices, you sense another presence, and then you feel yourself being moved. You hear the trap door close, the sound of voices becoming louder.

Sample Question: What do the voices want with you?

Variation: While reading a book you find yourself being pulled in between the pages and into the story.

Adaptation for Young Children: Have children hypothesize about what is under the secret trap door, the magic trap door in their basement, or perhaps under their house.

TINY VISION

Objective: **To develop a sense of individual impact on others.**

Premise: You and your best friend are walking along. You look down and see you have kicked a small furry, puffy, creature. (You think it is an insect.) The creature shouts at you like a human. It flies up, bites you in the eye and buzzes off. You writhe in pain while your friend rushes to get some water to wash out your eye. When he returns you have recovered somewhat. You look up at your friend and he suddenly begins to shrink until finally, he is only two inches tall. You run to get help. You knock on a door and a woman answers. When you look at her she also shrinks to a height of two inches.

Sample Questions: How will this affect your life? How can you use the power for good? How can you regain normal vision?

Variation: Your look makes people grow ten feet tall or your look gives them a disease.

Adaptation for Young Children: Have children pretend they are only two inches tall and pantomime their experiences.

PLANT POWER

Objective: **To broaden ideas about the possible things that could happen to any individual.**

Premise: It's a strange world. You realize this when you wake up one day to find a tree, a bush, and several other plants in your bedroom. You wake up fully and find you are being held hostage by walking, talking, violent plants.

Sample Questions: How are you being held? (by what power?) Why are they holding *you*? What are their plans for you?

Variation: Have the children pretend to be the plant leader and write an autobiography.

Adaptation for Young Children: Have the children draw and describe how different plants would move if they could somehow propel themselves.

THE INVISIBLE PERSON

Objective: To understand more fully how important it is to notice people and to be noticed.

Premise: You are always being told that you are getting too few vitamins. One day you find a new vitamin bottle on the table marked "vitamin ZIP4U8." You decide to take the whole bottle. You feel great but the next day you go to school (to town, to the store) and realize no one is speaking to you. You find no one sees you and no one hears you. You look down at yourself and discover you are invisible. You try to touch yourself and realize you can't be felt. You are a spirit.

Sample questions: How will you make your presence felt? How could you get back to normal? How will you decide if you want to become visible again?

Variations:
1. Everyone else becomes invisible to you. You can hear them but not see them.
2. You can be seen but have no physical substance. You can walk through a wall for example.

Adaptation for Young Children: Have children role play things they could do while invisible. Have them make a list of things invisible people could do that visible people cannot.

REMOVABLE SKIN

Objective: To increase risk-taking speculation.

Premise: While walking in the woods you meet an old woman and she winks at you. Suddenly you feel an itching. The itching leads to more itching. As you start to scratch you notice a common ordinary button right on your skin. You touch it and realize it comes undone. Right below is another button, and then another!

Sample Questions: What should you do, unbutton your skin and risk what may happen?

Variation:
1. You have just unbuttoned yourself and your outer skin has shed like a caterpillar's. What are you like now? What would make you take the chance?
2. You discover a zipper or a wind up key on everyone else's back. on a friends back

Adaptation for Young Children: Have the children pantomime the body buttons being found. Have them make up a nursery rhyme using "Humpty Dumpty" as a model.

"Squeezing time" is a teacher occupation and it usually means something is left out. However teachers forget that a single shared experience or topic can be the key to nearly every source of learning.

On the following page is a complex-looking diagram. It is really a simple mind-spring trick playing out various relationships. It begins in the center with a key experience area—"children's pets." Surrounding this are several general areas of study (e.g., "music," "art"). Then, for each subject area the diagram charts related learning interests and directions of inquiry that could be pursued. Some but not all the relationships are indicated with connecting lines. Teachers or children might like to try building a mind-spring association chart like this for other experiences such as—well, here are a dozen of the infinite possibilities.

1. A trip to the zoo
2. A visit by a foreign visitor
3. A walk in a park
4. The farm
5. The school itself
6. A holiday
7. A particular month or day of the week
8. Clocks and time
9. Summer vacation
10. A special story or poem
11. A picture or object that fascinates children
12. A new person in the school.

CREATIVE RISKS

Creative behavior in children has been closely linked to willingness to take risks. This is probably due to the fact that acting in creative ways demands self-confidence and security. Taking chances is easier when the individual is not concerned about the consequences. That is, if someone feels he cannot accept whatever happens as a result of what he does, that he will not be truly hurt, he is willing to take risks.

Risk taking also probably reflects an optimism that things will turn out well most of the time, at least, eventually, with enough sustained effort. This may be based on a history of success or at least of sufficiently good feelings and feedback from past efforts.

There follow five lists of possible personal risks—two for teachers, two for children, and one for both. These are set up as "personal brainstorming" exercises. For each suggested risk, the individual is asked to quickly assess as many independent conditions as possible under which he/she would take the risk or not take the risk. It might also be enjoyable to add items to this list of risks.

OUT-OF-SCHOOL TEACHER RISKS

Make a list of the conditions under which you would take each of the following risks. Try to list at least five or more independent conditions for each. Then reverse the procedure and list conditions under which you would *not* take the risk. You may think of many other risks.

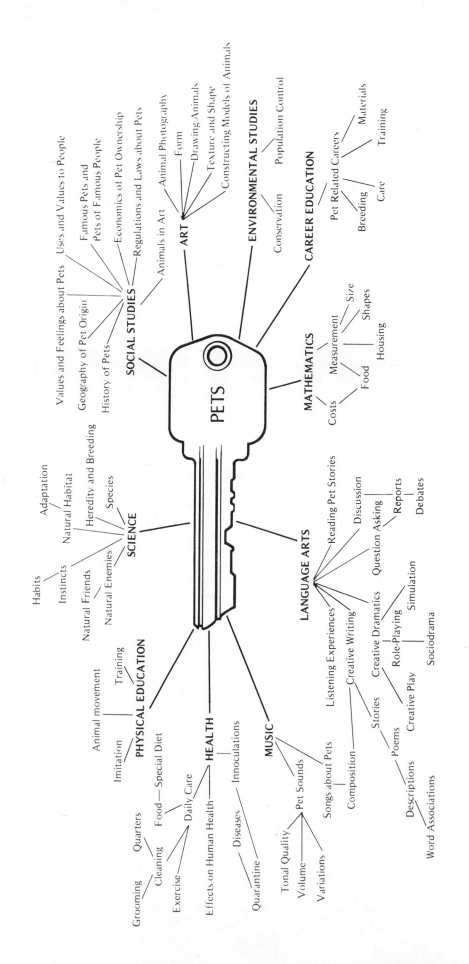

PETS

SOCIAL STUDIES
- Values and Feelings about Pets
- Uses and Values to People
- Geography of Pet Origin
- History of Pets
- Famous Pets and Pets of Famous People
- Economics of Pet Ownership
- Regulations and Laws about Pets
- Animals in Art

ART
- Animal Photography
- Form
- Drawing Animals
- Texture and Shape
- Constructing Models of Animals

ENVIRONMENTAL STUDIES
- Conservation
- Population Control

CAREER EDUCATION
- Pet Related Careers
  - Breeding
  - Care
  - Materials
  - Training

MATHEMATICS
- Measurement
  - Size
  - Shapes
  - Housing
  - Food
- Costs

LANGUAGE ARTS
- Reading Pet Stories
- Discussion
- Question Asking
- Reports
- Debates
- Listening Experiences
- Creative Writing
- Creative Dramatics
- Role-Playing
- Simulation
- Sociodrama
- Stories
- Creative Play
- Poems
- Descriptions
- Word Associations
- Composition

SCIENCE
- Habits
- Instincts
- Natural Friends
- Natural Enemies
- Adaptation
- Natural Habitat
- Heredity and Breeding
- Species

PHYSICAL EDUCATION
- Training
- Animal movement
- Imitation

HEALTH
- Food—Special Diet
- Daily Care
- Exercise
- Effects on Human Health
- Diseases
- Innoculations
- Quarantine
- Grooming
- Quarters
- Cleaning

MUSIC
- Pet Sounds
- Songs about Pets
- Tonal Quality
- Volume
- Variations

34

1. Bet two dollars on a horse race or ball game.
2. Drive the wrong way on a one-way street.
3. Go into a hospital contagious ward.
4. Walk up to a growling, snarling dog and pet it.
5. Eat an unfamiliar food without knowing its ingredients.
6. Invite a stranger into your home.
7. Try a new restaurant.
8. Buy a product without a recognizable brand name.
9. Park in a tow-away zone.
10. Loan money to an acquaintance.
11. Quit a job without having a new job waiting.
12. Buy clothes that are too tight.
13. Get a new kind of pet.
14. Buy something from a street peddler.
15. Try an unfamiliar route while traveling.
16. Offer help to a stranger in distress.
17. Start on a long trip without knowing your destination.
18. Take in a new family member.
19. Knowingly write a check for more money than you have.
20. Refuse to pay a bill.
21. Enter a contest.
22. Go to a new place to get your hair cut.
23. Try a new sport having an element of danger (such as sky diving or mountain climbing).
24. Move to a new neighborhood.
25. Go to a social event where you do not know anyone.

IN-SCHOOL TEACHER RISKS

The same rules apply for brainstorming about taking risks in school. First try to list five or more independent conditions under which you would do each of the following. Then try to list five conditions under which you would not.

1. Order a new class text without having seen it.
2. Order new materials without approval.
3. Change texts.
4. Make assignments without reading through them.
5. Change your basic routine for each teaching day.
6. Put all troublemakers in one group.
7. Argue with the principal.
8. Offer to work with another teacher.
9. Have students make the rules.
10. Try leaving a problem learner alone for a whole day.
11. Visit a student's home unannounced.
12. Ignore a discipline problem.
13. Not report an absentee.
14. Teach a controversial topic or point of view.
15. Write a letter to the school board.
16. Ask for an evaluation of administrators by teachers.
17. Request that your teaching be evaluated.
18. Give lower grades than children normally receive.

19. Teach a lesson differently than you taught it before.
20. Give the same test to several different classes.
21. Be late for school or leave early.
22. Bring up a question or an idea at a faculty meeting that will make the meeting longer.
23. Stand up for a child against another teacher in an argument.
24. Allow your class to be noisy.
25. Personally take the blame without excuse for a student's failure or problem.

IN-SCHOOL CHILD RISKS

Ask children to think about and discuss their own risk taking. Again the first task is to list five conditions under which the risk would be taken. Once this is done the conditions under which the risk would not be taken may prove equally interesting.

1. Raise your hand when you are not sure of the answer.
2. Ask a question about something you are supposed to know.
3. Turn homework in late.
4. Try to spell a word you don't know on the test.
5. Make an oral report.
6. Show something you have made to the class.
7. Interrupt the teacher.
8. Take something you have written to the teacher when it was not assigned.
9. Argue with the teacher.
10. Read aloud a story you have written.
11. Work with a group as a leader.
12. Tell the teacher or your friends about an idea you have for an invention.
13. Ask to have a paper of yours put on the bulletin board or ask that one not be put up.
14. Ask the teacher for a project that has not been returned.
15. Look for a new book in the library.
16. Go to school later than you are supposed to.
17. Volunteer for a project.
18. Ask the teacher for extra work.
19. Enter a spelling bee.
20. Try out for a part in a class play.
21. Demonstrate a new stunt in gym class.
22. Tell a story in front of the class.
23. Go to the principal's office.
24. Turn in a project early.
25. Ask a teacher to visit your parents.

OUT-OF-SCHOOL CHILD RISKS

1. Tell your friends you like school.
2. Ask your parents to help you with an assignment.
3. Get into a fight with someone bigger and stronger.
4. Play a new game.
5. Bring a new pet home without asking.
6. Show either of your parents a story or poem you have written.

7. Tell your parents about an idea you have.
8. Tell your parents about something important you have lost or broken.
9. Tell your parents about a problem you had in school.
10. Tell a friend a secret about yourself that you are ashamed of.
11. Eat something you have never tried before.
12. Go into a strange house.
13. Walk through a graveyard at night.
14. Explore in the woods.
15. Enter an area posted "No Trespassing."
16. Sleep in the woods alone.
17. Use something that belongs to your father or mother.
18. Tell somebody that you like them.
19. Ask someone if they like you.
20. Go on a kids' quiz show as a contestant.
21. Spend the night at a new friend's house.
22. Run away from home.
23. Apply for a part-time job.
24. Go home later than you are supposed to.
25. Spend all your money on one thing.

FANTASY RISKS

These risks no one would ever take because they would not have the opportunity. But suppose the opportunity did arise. What would keep you from taking the risk or prompt you to take it? Many of these examples are taken from myths, legends, and fiction.

1. Steal a magician's magic wand.
2. Enter a giant's house.
3. Work a magic spell in a sorcerer's book.
4. Dive headfirst into a cloud.
5. Ride a magic carpet.
6. Fight a dragon.
7. Enter a flying saucer.
8. Converse with a talking bear.
9. Follow a witch at night.
10. Ride on a winged horse.
11. Sprinkle pixie dust on yourself and fly.
12. Sleep in a haunted house.
13. Drink a magic potion.
14. Fly to outerspace in a spaceship.
15. Climb across a giant spider web.
16. Eat a mushroom that makes you shrink or grow.
17. Go through the looking glass to the world on the other side.
18. Grab hold of an angry leprechaun.
19. Enter a time machine.
20. Interrupt the fairy king's wedding.
21. Ride on a giant bee's back.
22. Buy a cursed object.
23. Use a magic wand.
24. Make three wishes granted by a golden fish.
25. Climb a glass mountain.

Creative Writing

PICTURE THIS

Objective: To help children project beyond the immediately apparent; to perceive that, though a picture may be worth many words, it is the imagination that mirrors what cannot be pictured.

Materials: A large box containing pictures of people, animals, objects, scenes.

Procedure: Have each child choose two or three pictures and write a story about them.

Variations:
1. Use only pictures of people talking and have the child write what they are thinking and saying.
2. Use only pictures of objects or the objects themselves. Have the children pretend to be the object (a football, the classroom doorknob) and write about a day in the existence of that object. They might write about an incident that the object witnessed.
3. Put the pictures in mystery envelopes and mix them up in a large box. Conduct a class drawing and have each child make a selection.
4. Mix up stories and pictures alternately, letting children guess which picture goes with which story.

BIG BREW IN BOSTON

Objective: To help children understand the importance of viewpoint in reported events.

Procedure: Give children the following directions: "Pretend that you are a free-lance newspaper writer at the time of the Boston Tea Party. You have to cover the story for newspapers in five different cities: Boston, Charleston, South Carolina, London, Paris and Madrid. Remembering that the event will have a different meaning and importance to people in each of these cities, try to write five different headlines."

Variations:
1. Have children write headlines for a series of events (such as those leading up to the American Revolution).
2. Suggest that they write some of the headlines that might have appeared if newspapers had been invented at the time of the ancient Egyptian or Roman empires.
3. Let them write headlines for the "historical" events that have happened in your school.

THE ZOOSTERS UNION

Objective: To help children make voting decisions based on the necessary qualifications for a particular job rather than popularity alone.

Procedure: Each student pretends to be his favorite zoo animal. Then each child must nominate members for a grievance committee that will represent the animals. Each child writes a paragraph about each nominee telling why he feels the animal nominated would be a good member. Then have children brainstorm in small groups to make a list of grievances to give to the committee. In their nominations and their grievances children are encouraged to think like the animal character they represent. (A cat would not nominate a dog, for example.)

Variations:
1. Form other zoo committees (one for a party, one to investigate "alleged" crimes of the king of beasts, etc.).
2. Have children imagine their favorite entertainers as animals and explain why they chose the particular animals.

DEAR AGGRAVATED

Objective: **To develop problem-solving skills.**

Procedure: Let the children pretend they are writers of an advice column for a newspaper and have them write answers to problems submitted by their classmates. (These problems can be written and placed in a box from which the children draw the ones they will answer.)

Variations:
1. Cut out actual letters (minus the answers) from the columns of well-known advice columnists.
2. Let the children pretend to be other newspaper columnists (e.g., a celebrity columnist writing about the "famous people" in the class).
3. Rewrite those advice columns or "how to do it tips" which appear in the daily newspapers and that the students do not agree with.

WHICH HOLIDAY?

Objective: **To develop the ability to identify with and sympathize with other people and their ideas.**

Procedure: Have children pretend they are a day of the year—a certain holiday. Let them write a short paragraph about how they would feel the day before and/or after their particular holiday. Let the class guess the holiday.

Variation: As the holiday, let children describe how they believe they ought to be celebrated.

STRINGING

Objective: **To develop the ability to interpret imaginatively.**

Materials: String, paint, construction paper.

Procedure: Have the children take a piece of construction paper and fold it in half. Next, have them dip the string in paint and place it between the folds. Then pull the string around, unfold the paper, and discard the string. Give students time to study their paintings. Then have them describe what they see.

Variations:
1. Display the paintings and have the children write what they see in different pupils' work.
2. Have children make a list of the many different things they see in their art.

NEW LAW

Objective: **To help children conceptualize the need for law and for changes in the law.**

Procedure: Give children the following suggestion in written form. "Pretend you are a member of Congress. Write a law that we need in our country today."

Variations:
1. Send this new law (in the form of a bill) through the proper channels for becoming actual law. Have half of the class be the Senate and the other half the House. One person acts as president. Let each child write a justification for his or her law. See how many of the bills become law.
2. Have the children make a law for governing the class.
3. Have each child pretend to be the president and explain how he or she would enforce the law.
4. Have the children write funny or ridiculous laws.

FORTUNE COOKIE WRITING

Objective: **To help children learn predictive skills. To develop an understanding of broad general statements.**

Materials: Bag of fortune cookies.

Procedure: Have children eat the cookies and share their fortune with the class. Then have each child write his or her own fortune to put in a cookie.

Variations:
1. Write the fortunes in dialect.
2. Prepare new messages for candy valentine hearts.
3. Have children write horoscopes for the zodiac signs.
4. Have children write historical fortunes for characters from the past concerning what was about to happen to them.

PERFECT PERSON

Objective: **To help children clarify their conceptions of themselves as ideal individuals.**

Procedure: The students are to write a story describing the perfect individual (include abilities, physical attributes, talents). This can be someone the student admires or would like to be, a real person or imaginary, but should be someone with humanly possible traits.

Variations:
1. The child can select a personality (historical or modern or both) as her ideal and tell why.
2. Have the children create a fantasy person with unreal traits.

   Height _____
   Weight _____
   Color eyes _____
   Color hair _____
   Special physical features _____
   Special abilities _____
   Character traits _____
   Best friends _____

MYSELF

Objective: **To develop summary abilities and to help children to know themselves better.**

Procedure: Have each child write one sentence that describes himself as a person.

Variation: Have the child write a rhyming couplet (or suggest another stanzaic form) describing himself.

ME AND YOU

Objective: **To help children develop a stronger self-image.**

Procedure: Have the children draw, diagram, sketch, or "doodle" a composite picture of how they perceive themselves. They may use pencil, pen and ink, or paint. Some children may prefer modeling clay or cutting pictures from a magazine or newspaper and pasting them on a sheet of paper. They do not use words.

On the back of the same paper or by creating another model, have them make a composite of how they think their class or group perceives them. Do not allow them to look at the first model while working on the second. Compare the two and discuss them with the class. After several weeks, repeat the process without reference to the first attempt. Children can compare the two sets by writing about them.

Variation: Give the children a form on which to structure their composite—such as a coat-of-arms shield, a totem pole, a collage poster—with each part standing for definite aspects of their life or character.

WHAT DO YOU HEAR?

Objective: **To develop listening skills.**

Procedure: Take the children on a listening walk around the school grounds. They must listen carefully to the sounds they hear. Then have each child pretend he is some "thing" outside and write about what sounds this "thing" hears. For example, write about the sounds an ant hears.

Variation: Have children write about loud sounds pretending these are very soft.

THE MUSIC SAID...

Objective: **To explore the contribution of sound to our sense of mood and sequence.**

Materials: Records (good example, "Peter and the Wolf").

Procedure: Have the children listen to the music carefully. Then have them write the story expressed by the music. They might want to discuss the recording before writing. Have the children try to do the same thing with a series of sound effects.

Variation: Have children doodle words as the music plays. Then have them write a paragraph describing the mood the music created.

LET'S WRITE A NUMBER

Objective: **To help children realize that values, however small, are attached to everything.**

Procedure: Have the children write a number that means love; one that means bad luck; one that means magic. Have them make a shape to signify this virtue, quality, or idea and put the number in it. Then they can write a story about how the number got its meaning.

Variation: Have the children write a fable or short story telling why the number they chose means love, honesty, etc.

COMMUNICATION WITH SOUNDS

Objective: **To develop greater awareness of the pervasiveness of auditory messages.**

Materials: Tape recorded sounds usually associated with conveying messages: policeman's whistle, cheering crowds, ringing alarm clock, siren, or clapping.

Procedure: Play the recording and have pupils identify the sound and the message. Then have them choose various sounds to use in telling a story—just sounds, and then write a story about the sounds.

Variation: Have the children write a story in which the sounds signify a different meaning than they do normally.

IT FEELS LIKE . . .

Objective: **To understand the relationship between tactile and verbal experience.**

Materials: A large bag with nonhardening clay inside. (One bag is needed for each child. The child should not be able to see through the bag.)

Procedure: The children begin by putting their hands in the bag and making something out of the clay without peeking in the bag. They remove the bags and write about the sculpture.

Variation: Let the children label their classmates' sculptures and afterwards compare the labels.

SMELLER TELLER

Objective: **To develop greater sensory awareness.**

Procedure: Have children use their sense of smell to aid in writing a story. Ask them to think of objects that they have smelled that could tell an interesting story such as, a cedar chest, a bar of soap, paint, or a pine forest. A story about a pine forest, for example, might concern a dangerously threatening fire or a group of vacationing campers.

Variations:
1. Have the children list hungry smells, or sweet smells or sour smells.
2. Have the children pretend to take a blindfolded journey, and then write a narrative description of only the sounds and smells they encounter. Have the other children try to guess the places they have been.

IDEAL WORLD RECIPE

Objective: **To help children analyze ideals and feelings.**

Procedure: Have the children prepare a recipe for some abstract quality like peace, happiness, freedom, or justice.

Example: Peace Stew
Begin with a sense of awe and love for the Creator. Blend two parts understanding with two parts of love for fellow human beings. Mix well with generous portions of sensitivity. Add a willingness to share. Put in a dash of humor, pour into an empty world and allow to slowly simmer until everyone feels it in their hearts.

Variations:
1. Have the children write recipes for other human conditions such as a broken heart, or the perfect marriage.
2. Have the children write recipes for physical feelings.
3. Instead of recipes have the children write prescriptions.

FAMOUS PEOPLE

Objective: To help children understand the importance of heroes and heroines in our culture.

Procedure: There are many stories about famous people that probably are not true, but were made up by people who saw in these individuals a quality they respected (George Washington and the cherry tree—honesty; Robert Bruce and the spider—persistence; the devil and Daniel Webster—courage and humility). Have the children choose a famous figure from the list below and make up a story about him/her that illustrates some particular character trait.

Susan B. Anthony
Shirley Chisolm
John Kennedy
Andrew Jackson
Daniel Boone
Neil Armstrong
Clara Barton

Martin Luther King
Chief Joseph
Harriet Tubman
Jim Thorpe
Billy Jean King
Will Rogers
William Tell

Variation: Have the children write a "what if" story about a decision their famous person could have made differently to change the course of his/her life.

MIXING MATH AND WORDS

Objective: To make verbal problem solving more meaningful.

Procedure: Let the children make up story problems for math. They can have the other children solve the problems.

Variation: Have children rewrite word problems in their arithmetic books so they make more sense to them.

FEELING FUNNY WORDS

Objective: To help children visualize relationships between words and their meanings.

Materials: A list of words that convey physical or emotional meanings. *Examples:* scary, shaky, drunk, tremendous, tiny, long.

Procedure: Ask the students to write the words so that they visually convey their meanings.

Variation: Have the children play a guessing game showing one letter of their word at a time until someone can discover what the word is.

SLANGING IT

Objective: To help children in adapting their written language to particular purposes.

Procedure: Have the children create a story using the slang expressions of a particular era or group of people (the 1950s, musicians, C.B.'ers). It would be a good idea to have children prepare a slang word list first. Have them rewrite a familiar story such as a fairy tale and put it into slang.

Variation: Have children create their own slang dictionary, listing and defining 10 to 20 words.

CREATURE ZOO

Objective: To develop a more adaptive imagination.

Materials: Colored paper, roll paper.

Procedure: Have each child make a "crazy creature" from the colored paper. Torn paper or cut paper art technique can be used. Then paste them on the long roll and title it "Our _____ Creature Zoo." (Fill in the blank according to the type of creatures made.) Have each child make up a name for his creature, and write a story about him. Include information concerning his looks, sex (male/female), size, personality (friendly/fierce), and his habits.

Variation: Use alternate themes such as "Our Horror Castle," "Our _____ Creature Circus."

"I MEAN...."

Objective: To develop appreciation of the importance of word selection in communication and to increase vocabulary.

Procedure: Have the children write a "Norm Crosby" type story. The purpose is to substitute the wrong, yet right sounding word for the correct term.

Variations: The children could swap stories and try to fill in the correct words.

STORY RECIPE

Objective: To develop the ability to perceive and build relationships among diverse elements.

Materials: Mixing bowl, wooden spoon, and pieces of paper with the ingredients for stories on them (characters, locations, descriptions, plot sequences).

Procedure: Instruct the children to draw out several story ingredients and place them in the mixing bowl. Then toss gently and see what story they can write with the combination.

VARIATIONS AND THEME

Objective: **To develop skills in rewriting for a particular purpose.**

Materials: Any reading material.

Procedure: Have children rewrite reading materials changing the level of difficulty. This can build expansion, elaboration, and descriptive skills as well as the ability to summarize and edit. Start with a poem or some other short selection. For example, "Sally ran to school" can be expanded to "Sally raced breathlessly into the elementary school building."

Variation: Have the children try to alter the mood or the setting of the reading selection. Hopefully they will be able to see how these factors affect the story's development.

RELIEF WRITING

Objective: **To help children realize that writing can serve as an emotional outlet.**

Procedure: Give the children these directions. "Start writing about yourself. Express your angers, hostilities, loves, or despairs by describing how you feel. Keep writing as fast as possible. Don't worry about sentences or spelling. Always try to express exactly how you feel. Relive your inward feelings on paper. After you finish, destroy the paper if you want. The experience can be timed and might be followed with a discussion about how it made the children feel.

Variation: Use happiness, joy, hope, and ambition.

FAVORITE FOODS

Objective: **To develop in children an awareness of the qualities of things they like and dislike.**

Procedure: The children are to write riddles about their favorite food. The riddle should include where the food comes from, how it looks, what it does for you, how it tastes, how it is made. Have the class guess the answers.

Variations: 1. Have the children pretend to be their favorite food and describe (in poetry or prose) their feelings and ideas. This can be done for food they dislike also.
2. Have the children pretend to be the food they hate most or a food they have never tried.

Example: What is:
> green
> crisp
> juicy
> sour
> taste good on a hamburger?

IF I HAD NAMED IT

Objective: **To develop the ability to label objects and ideas in many different ways.**

Procedure: Discuss metaphors. Tell the children they are going to give things different names (e.g., cloud—fluffy white pillow). Think about things that are in the air, on land, and under the water. Each child then writes at least one metaphor for land, one for water, and one for air.

Examples: In the air—bird—swiftly moving comma
On the land—mushroom—umbrella for elves
Under the water—sea urchin—cactus that crawls

WHO LIVES IN THE ATTIC?

Objective: **To develop skill in drawing inferences.**

Materials: A picture of a cluttered old attic (with lots of junk in it).

Procedure: Have the children look at this picture and think of some creatures that might live there (fantasy creatures preferably). Draw a picture of what these creatures might look like and give them a name. Now write an adventure story about them.

Variations:
1. Write about what these creatures eat, how they entertain themselves, who their friends and enemies are.
2. Use other storage and disposal areas (basements, garage, garbage dumps, crawl spaces, junkyards).

PICTURE WRITING

Objective: **To help children understand the relationship between thinking and writing.**

Procedure: Have children write short stories in the form of a rebus or in Indian picture writing. For the former, they must realize that the pictures refer to both the meaning and the sound of words. In Indian picture writing an eye may stand for the word "I" or syllable "i".

Variation: Have children use number codes to write stories.

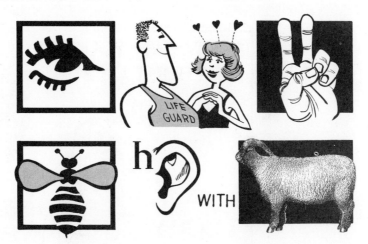

LET'S GET ALONG TOGETHER

Objective: **To develop the ability to reason out differences of opinion.**

Procedure: After several children have had a misunderstanding, have them argue the matter out on paper, listing their complaints and grievances.

Variations:
1. Have each child take the other person's point of view in the argument.
2. Have each child select a spokesperson.

SCRAMBLE BOARD

Objective: **To develop perceptual skills.**

Procedure: Make use of a scramble board for spelling drills. Have students find and circle spelling words on the scramble board. After the word is located the student pronounces the word and then spells it.

1. Police
2. Animal
3. Elephant
4. Robber
5. Bloat
6. Plain

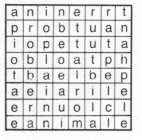

Variations:
1. Have the children make up their own scramble board from a word list.
2. Hide a sentence giving directions to the child in the scramble.

55

MADISON AVENUE

Objective: **To help the children understand the elements of advertising.**

Procedure: Have students design an advertising campaign for a product with a nonsense name. This can include commercials for television, billboards, magazines, newspaper spreads, along with other promotional gimmicks.

Variation: Have the students redesign the advertising campaign for a currently popular product.

SUPER SOUNDS

Objective: **To help children become more aware of the infinitely detailed and beautiful world they live in.**

Procedure: There are sounds around us that are so quiet we cannot hear them—an ant crawling, a leaf or snowflake falling, a butterfly flapping its wings, etc. Have children think of as many quiet sounds as they can and have them write them down.

Variation: Make a list of other kinds of sounds made by imaginary things, scary things, kind things.

NEW VERSE FOR THE SONG

Objective: **To develop skills in understanding poetic form and to increase sensitivity to the lyricism and mood of poetry.**

Procedure: Have the children write new verses to their favorite songs. These verses must be consistent with the song in theme, metric pattern, and rhythm. A few suggested songs: "My Country Tis of Thee"; "Jesus Loves Me"; "Row Row Row Your Boat" (also include currently popular songs).

Variations: 1. Have the children "translate" the lyrics of currently popular songs (the top 20) into language that their parents can understand.
2. Children could also explain the song's main idea in a single sentence or give the song a new title.

STORY TRAIN

Objective: **To develop skill in combining story elements.**

Materials: Make a chart of a toy train (engine and four cars). Glue the engine on, but just glue the cars on three sides. This forms a pocket in which cards may be inserted.

First Car—Story Problems

Had a flat tire
Has no friends
Has no shoes

Second Car—Traits

Tall
Mean
Funny

Third Car—Character

King
Elf
Elephant

Fourth Car—Location

At a movie
On a horse
In school

Procedure: Insert these cards in the proper pockets. The children must draw one card from each pocket and complete a story weaving together the story elements described on their cards.

Variations:
1. Cars can be added for additional characters, color words, objects, and other elements.
2. Two trains can be used, one representing fantasy problems, characters, etc., and the other realistic.

MAKING A NEW FRIEND

Objective: **To help children learn to build plot structures appropriate to character.**

Materials: Biographical sketch cards giving the brief history and description of some new imagined friend. (These can be prepared by children in a previous writing assignment.)

Examples:
1. Horace has blonde hair, green eyes, and freckles. He is eight years old. He lives with his grandmother and his pet pig, Uriwinkle. He brought the pig from the country to the city. Horace used to live in the country. He speaks pig.
2. Marvene is nine years old. She has a problem because she turns invisible on Tuesdays. But the rest of the week she is fine. On Tuesdays, only her eyebrows show and even her clothes turn invisible. This has always disturbed her teachers especially on Tuesdays when Marvene is supposed to lead the lunch line.
3. Halberette is ten. She is a marvelous mechanic who not only takes things apart but also puts them together. When she puts things together, though, they often run differently than they did before.

Procedure: Give each child a biographical sketch card and have him make up a story about an adventure he and this imaginary friend have together.

Variation: The child may make up the biographical sketch himself. Or each child may exchange his biographical sketch with others.

RUB THE MAGIC LAMP

Objective: **To help children clarify and explore their own desires and aspirations.**

Materials: A gravy boat or some other object that the children can pretend is a magic lamp.

Procedure: Create an atmosphere of mystery and magic by describing the many wishes the lamp has fulfilled. Brainstorm with the children a list of incantatory magic words to be used when invoking the lamp's mysterious power. Allow each child to rub the magic lamp and chant the magic words while making a wish. Have them write a story about this wish.

Variation: Have the children write stories about similarly fantastic or mysterious objects possessing strange powers. Their stories could focus on a magic wand for example that changes somebody into something, or a musical instrument that charms animals to obey commands.

Oral activities in the classroom make teachers very quickly aware of individual differences in children. Shy, withdrawn, vivacious, aggressive, or boisterous children all assert their differences and express their individuality in oral communication. The difficulties teachers èxperience in meeting individual needs while concurrently moving toward instructional goals are patently and immediately obvious in speaking and listening activities.

Much of what goes on in the school day involves oral activity of some type. This is as it should be for speaking and listening are the most common forms of daily communication for most people. Commonly, people talk more than they write and listen more than they read. The media of television and radio have done much to create a fantasy world of one-way oral communication. But two-way, active verbal interaction continues to dominate real life.

Oral activities of one kind or another afford many opportunities to develop important skills.

A. Report and speech making require skills in:

1. Preparing and organizing
2. Working from notes and outlines
3. Using visual aides
4. Mastering information
5. Convincing and arguing
6. Gaining and holding audience interest

Of course giving reports and making speeches involve many other skills, but these represent only a few of the more crucial ones upon which teaching should focus.

B. Discussion involves skills relating to:

1. Ideating
2. Question asking and inquiry
3. Question answering and response
4. Evaluation
5. Synthesis and analysis
6. Mastery and application of information and concepts

Discussion takes many forms: debate, class interaction or class meeting, evaluation, debriefing sessions, question and answer periods, panel presentation and interaction, problem-solving small group sessions, brainstorming, and many others.

C. Dramatization and choral reading require skills in verbal and nonverbal expression, comprehension and interpretation of the written word, vocal projection, and following directions among others.

D. Creative dramatics take several forms. These overlap each other and no clear distinctions are possible. However, the following types of dramatics might be categorized.

1. Dramatic play, or the natural play of children in which they act out situations familiar to them, often assuming the roles of people with whom they identify. These may have no plot and no noticeable beginning or end.
2. Sociodrama, or acting out a problem situation.

3. Role play, or dramatically interpreting what someone else (or something else) might do, think, feel, and say in reaction to a stimulus situation, or problem. Roles may be of specific people or of types of people.

4. Docu-drama, or acting out a real situation or event that has already occurred and has a known outcome.

5. Psychodrama, or acting out personally relevant problems about which there are no predetermined solutions.

6. Structured drama, or dramatic interpretation of written plot sequences and dialogue. Structured dramatics takes many forms.

   a. Storytelling or describing and recounting a series of events to an audience. The events may be true, fictionalized, or a combination of both. The storyteller may invent or borrow stories. The ultimate purpose is the benefit and enjoyment of the audience.

   b. Simulation or enactment of processes and problems following a prescribed series of steps, or in game situations, a prescribed set of rules and procedures. There is little opportunity for emotive role involvement and the main purpose is better understanding of the process concept being simulated.

   c. Story play or the enactment of a story plot line. This is done without script and is event and character centered rather than script centered.

   d. Dramatic reading and oral interpretation of plays, poems, and other forms of writing.

   e. Theatrical play making—the development for presentation to an audience of a prepared script, including memorization of parts and action.

   f. Singing—the musical interpretation of ideas and feelings. Cantata, musical comedy, opera, and operetta represent refined and sophisticated forms.

ADVICE FOR TEACHING AND ENCOURAGING CREATIVE ORAL EXPRESSION

A number of suggestions are offered here to the teacher who is attempting to utilize the various forms of creative oral expression in the classroom.

1. Encourage children to experiment with expressing themselves orally by saying things using different inflections and expressions.

2. Concentrate on one or two limited areas of oral communication at a time. Do not try to develop pronunciation, inflection, projection, timing, gesture, position and facial expression—all at once.

3. Encourage preparation by providing practice time, giving children the chance to rehearse their parts and repeat their lines.

4. Set mood and atmosphere by offering verbal descriptions, by supplying background information and encouraging prop and scenery design or construction.

5. Minimize distractions even during rehearsals. Concentration and involvement are most important in these times.

6. Record children and let them listen to themselves. Then if possible, let them repeat the activity making changes.

7. Provide a way for students to step into and out of roles so that they can be observers and interpreters of themselves. A "magic" circle can be useful here—one into which the children step to act.

8. Keep it simple. Work on limited material with a limited number of children to begin with. Keep it under control until the children's (and the teacher's) capabilities can be explored and realistic limits set.

9. Work in short sessions—with breaks. Schedule these as often as possible and at the best available times in the day (when children are most alert).

10. Preface any difficult and intense oral activity with short preparatory warm-up sessions.

 **HUMPTY DUMPTY**

Objective: **To develop better understanding of the story element in poetry.**

Materials: A book of nursery rhymes colorfully illustrated.

Procedure: Have children discuss "magic" materials to put Humpty Dumpty together again so that if he had another fall he would not break. They might want to talk about whether modern glues and methods could put Humpty Dumpty back in shape or ways such falls could be prevented (a safety net, a seat belt on the wall). Then let the children act out the great fall and their own repair story. Several children can portray Humpty Dumpty in turn, each trying to show different situations causing the fall and ways of falling. They might want to involve a partner or a small group in this. (Reasonable care will have to be taken to prevent injury.)

Variations:
1. Try other nursery rhymes as sources for discussion and acting out exercises ("Hey Diddle Diddle," "Little Boy Blue," "Jack and Jill").
2. The original Mother Goose rhymes were full of political overtones. Older children might discuss currently popular or well-known figures in the news who could be identified with characters in the old nursery rhymes. This exercise could also serve as an impetus to writing new rhymes patterned on the Mother Goose model.

THE ANIMAL GAME

Objective: **To enhance awareness of variations in personality and mood.**

Procedure: Ask students to think of human characteristics for animals. What animal could be slow, lazy, irresolute, and indifferent? What animal could be nervous, energetic, inclined to rash decisions? What animal would be a star? What animal would be a good talker?

Give students a list of animals. Ask them to assign human traits to a "good" one and to a "bad" one.

rattlesnake	woodchuck
grizzly bear	squirrel
red fox	rabbit
puma	gray wolf
musk ox	elk
gorilla	mongoose

Have children act out the human traits they ascribe to the animals.

Variations:
1. Try the same activity with insects, birds, or fish.
2. Use only one type of animal (e.g., reptiles) and try to identify species which fit the traits.

CAMPAIGN SPEECHES

Objective: **To increase ability to understand political issues.**

Procedure: Give students the following stimulus description: "Pretend you are a potential candidate for President of the United States. Draft the political platform you would run on if you were neither a Democrat nor a Republican. Then prepare a campaign speech to give orally to the class."

Variation: Have children prepare the platform in a group and then have them choose one group member to give the speech. Have the others make a pitch for the candidate and appeal to several special interest groups (minority groups, professional groups, women's groups). Each group can take a turn pretending to be one of the special interest groups.

DRESSING UP A BOOK REPORT

Objective: **To deepen identification with fictional or historical characters as a means of better understanding human nature and motivation.**

Procedure: Dress up a book report assignment by having a costume chart with the following directions: "After reading your favorite book, dress as one of the characters and tell about yourself. Try to speak like the character but do not reveal his or her identity or the name of the book."

Variation: Fill a box with Halloween masks as well as simply made paper, papier-mâché, and paper bag masks. Give book reports wearing masks that recall characters in the book.

"THINGS I WOULD LIKE TO CHANGE" BOOK REPORTS

Objective: **To increase critical reading and evaluational abilities.**

Procedure: Include the following directions to children writing book reports:
"After reading your book, tell the class the things you disliked about the book and how you would like to change the story." Advise them of some specific kinds of things they may do; that is, leave out or add a character or a chapter, perhaps write an alternative ending.

Variation: Have children give a short talk about a question the book did not answer.

PROFESSIONAL PROBLEM

Objective: **To develop appreciation for the characteristic problems of specific professions.**

Procedure: Brainstorm with children a list of different and interesting professions. Have each student choose a profession and then describe the perils or problems of this profession.

Variation: Have children act out a hazard or a disagreeable aspect of their chosen profession.

DESCRIBE YOUR FRIEND

Objective: **To develop understanding of what makes a good friend.**

Procedure: Give children the following directions:

"Choose your best friend in the class.
1. Describe his/her good characteristics.
2. Tell about three things that you and your friend do together.
3. Name three things your friend likes to do without you."

Variation: Have children make up an invisible friend to tell about.

SHAPE GAME

Objective: **To develop descriptive power.**

Materials: Copies of various simple drawings such as line drawings, geometric figures, cartoons.

Procedure: Have children explain to a group without using their hands how this drawing should be drawn. (Start with simple geometric designs or special purpose buildings like barns, doghouses, silos, hotels, or historical buildings.)

Variation: Have children give verbal descriptions of patterns in fabric or wallpaper.

SUPER TEACHER

Objective: **To encourage classification of ideals.**

Materials: Wall chart or cassette recorder.

Procedure: Have children describe the perfect teacher! What should he or she be like? Each child in turn gives a sentence or two describing "super teacher." The sentences can be charted or recorded. Each child must add something new to the listed ideas. Then move to the concepts of "super student," or "super kid." Through discussion examine how the ideals for each of these are alike and how they differ.

Variation: Use other professions and occupations instead of teachers.

NONSENSE VOCABULARY

Objective: **To develop fluent verbal response skills.**

Procedure: Ask each student to make up his or her own rhyming vocabulary. Begin with simple repeats like chuckle, suckle, schnuckle, muckle, ruckle. Some interesting rhyme words:

orange	scooter	squirrel
purple	internal	democracy
Pluto	enamel	minus
soupy		

Variation: Use this exercise as an oral warm-up for more complex activities.

THE LAST CHOICE

Objective: To develop decision making skills.

Procedure: Have the children discuss the following problem playing the roles of these six characters: a doctor, lawyer, teacher, farmer, chemist, and an engineer. "We are the last six people left on earth. Our planet has been invaded by creatures from outer space. They want three volunteers to take back with them." Have the children decide among themselves who should go.

Variation: Have the children choose among these and other professions the three most likely to help in other problem situations such as: to aid trapped coal miners, to settle a labor union dispute, to build a house, to help a parent with a juvenile delinquent child, to help a county with a fuel shortage.

LET'S THINK IN COLOR

Objective: To become more observant and better able to describe details.

Procedure: Have each child think of a color but keep his or her choice a secret. In turn, the children name several objects in the room, on the street, etc. that have that color in them. Objects named may be somewhat vague. For example, the student may choose "money" for green, silver, or brown. The other children try to guess the color. The more subtle the choices, of course, the longer correct guesses can be delayed.

Variation: Try the same guessing game using simple geometric shapes or with things that make a particular type of sound (clicking, ringing, etc.)

FAMILY AFFAIRS

Objective: To clarify values in family relationships.

Materials: Magazines, catalogues, scissors, large flat box tops, paste.

Procedure: Instruct the children to think about the kind of family that they would like to have and ask them to cut out figures representing members of their ideal family from the magazines. After the family is assembled ask the children to make a house in a box top for their family to live in. This is an ideal home. Each child is to use their magazine and catalogue pictures to show the various rooms in the house. When the box top houses are complete, display them and have the children talk about their ideal home and family.

Variation: Have children plan an ordinary week for their ideal family, a special vacation, or a simple outing.

STRANGE THINGS FOR SALE

Objective: To develop descriptive power.

Materials: A box of nonsense objects which have interesting shapes. The shape though does not offer any clue to the function.

Procedure: Each child takes an object from the box keeping his or her eyes closed. They feel the object and then put it back in the box. Next, each one must attempt to sell the object by making up a promotional commercial.

Variations:
1. Have children pantomime using the object.
2. Have children draw strange and wonderful machines or small objects but leave them unlabeled. Trade them around to be sold in the commercial.

WHAT COULD THEY DO?

Objective: To increase powers of projective thinking.

Materials: Pictures of objects or the objects themselves.

Procedure: Show each object and have the children make up an oral short story about what the object might reveal if it could talk. Examples of objects: onion, trash can, chair, doorknob. This can be followed up with dramatizing or illustrating activities.

Variation: Pretend the objects were taken from some hypothetical or mythical location; e.g., a doctor's office, a king's palace, a factory.

THE STRANGE PINKINKIBLUES

Objective: To develop in children the ability to recognize prejudice in themselves and others.

Procedure: The Pinkinkiblues are five-legged, yellow, bald-headed people with mouths on both sides of their heads. They hate anything pink or blue. How do Pinkinkiblues celebrate their birthdays? What do they eat? What do they receive for presents? Make up a birthday song to sing to them. What would be the reaction of a Pinkinkiblue to a pink and blue present, to the sky on a sunny day, or to cotton candy? Do they also hate hairy things, two-legged things?

Variations:
1. Have children determine what problems a Pinkinkiblue would cause living in their neighborhood.
2. Have children determine ways to deal with Pinkinkiblues.

FIRST PERSON

Objective: **To increase ability to project ideas toward distant and very large objects.**

Materials: Maps of the solar system or the locations of stars might be useful stimuli.

Procedure: Have groups brainstorm a list of characteristics of two far distant planets. One of these planets should have realistic features while the other should have fantastic ones. Give each child one of the descriptions. Each student tells the rest of the class what she or he would do as the first person on that planet. They might explain how they would survive, what they would do first, how they would get off the planet, or how they would claim the planet.

Variation: Have the child pretend to be an inhabitant of the planet meeting his or her first earth visitor. Knowing what they do about earth would they want to make the earthling welcome?

CIVILIZATIONS OF PROBLEM SOLVERS

Objective: **To develop understanding of the commonality of the problems of human relationships.**

Procedure: Have the class identify a list of common, down-to-earth human relationship problems that they feel would exist in any time and place. Then have them play out the problems as they might have happened in different civilizations or cultures.

Examples of historical periods or civilizations:

cave man	American Revolution
ancient Rome	Civil War
Middle Ages	World War I
today in America	today

Problems might arise from situations such as:

different values between two individuals	crisis decisions
conflicts over home rules	parental disputes
disappointments	economic problems
values disagreements	

Variation: Have children discuss or dramatize the problem situations in different cultures of the modern world.

LOST CONTINENT

Objective: **To increase inventive ideation by removing limiting conventions and rules.**

Materials: As a preamble to this exercise students might be encouraged to read fictionalized or realistic accounts of previously uninhabited, or long lost islands.

Procedure: Have students discuss and speculate about a newly discovered imaginary continent. Ask them to describe its climate and its vegetation (including flowers, fruits, and vegetables). Also, have them list the animals that might inhabit this world and offer a short one-sentence oral description of each. If children have difficulty, have them try to combine unlikely features of known creatures (crocapillars, for instance would combine the characteristics of crocodiles with caterpillars).

Variation: Have the children describe prevailing conditions on the new continent with adjectives like "warm and friendly," "mysterious and frightening," "dangerous and perilous." Then any observations on the indigenous wildlife and vegetation should be consistent with this overall characterization.

Literary Stimuli: *The Mysterious Island, Robinson Crusoe,* and *The Swiss Family Robinson.*

THE BEING THERE GAME

Objective: **To encourage attention to detail and to increase visualization abilities.**

Procedure: This activity should come after an extensive in-depth study of some historic period or some other culture. Have a group of eight to ten children sit in a circle. All the children shut their eyes and set their imaginations to work. The teacher or an especially creative child begins describing a particular place or event (a colonial plantation, the battlefield at Gettysburg, an Indian dwelling) and everyone tries to imagine that they are on-the-scene observers. Each child describes a different aspect of the event or setting. They may describe what they see, smell, or what they hear. The teacher encourages total participation with questions such as: "What is hanging on the wall? What furniture is in the room? What sounds can you hear from outside? Is there someone standing nearby?"

Variation: Make the activity a guessing game by having the children describe a particular illustration they have seen relating to the topic.

TWIST AND TURN SCULPTURES

Objective: **To increase imaginative powers and the ability to project ideas.**

Materials: Pictures of modern sculptures. A sufficient number of pieces of wire or pipe cleaner and small pieces of Styrofoam for each child.

Procedure:
1. Staple one end of each of the wires to Styrofoam pieces for each child.
2. Ask the children to twist and turn the wire into any desired shape to make a kind of sculpture.
3. Have them name the sculpture and explain orally or in writing why it deserves its name. Display the sculptures.

Variation: Have children pretend that their sculptures have a practical function or purpose. Ask them to explain this usage.

IT WAS THERE

Objective: **To help in understanding the importance of perspective.**

Materials: Materials for children to make masks as well as assorted costumes, hats, and other props.

Procedure: Have each person pretend to be an object or part of something that was present at a particular event. Then let the students act out what event these objects would have witnessed. It is best to have children work in groups of three to five.

Examples of events and actors:
- Writing or signing the Declaration of Independence
  —a quill pen, a doorknob, a desk drawer, a handkerchief
- The first pony express delivery
  —a saddlebag, a bridle, the rider's hat, a letter
- The invention of the incandescent light bulb
  —various unsuccessful filaments, the light bulb
- The sinking of the Titanic
  —a ballroom chandelier, the side of the ship, a lifeboat, the captain's logbook.

Variations:
1. Use this technique as a method of reporting current events.
2. Make this an after-the-fact discussion among the "things."

THE CHAIN MAKER

Objective: To increase verbal fluency and ability to give a variety of responses to the same problem.

Materials: Cards containing the picture or name of a city helper such as policeman, fireman, garbage man, sanitation worker, ambulance driver.

Procedure: Have the children go through the following steps.

1. They form a circle or chain.
2. The teacher chooses a leader to begin.
3. The leader stands in the middle of the circle and holds up a card.
4. He/she points to someone who tells what the helper does for people.
5. Each time the same card is held up, a new way of helping must be given for that worker.
6. If someone cannot offer a new way, the chain is broken and that person goes to the inside of the circle.
7. The "broken" link earns his way back into the chain by giving a correct answer when another link becomes broken.

Variation: Follow the same procedure but for city helpers substitute household tools and utensils.

A STRANGE COMPANY

Objective: To develop group problem-solving skills.

Procedure: The class is divided into groups of six or seven. Each individual is asked to design a role for himself in terms of age, occupation, sex, race, and social status.

Example: *Age:* 26
Occupation: plumber
Sex: male
Race: Caucasian
Social traits: married, 2 children, income of $17,000 each year.

He or she does this independently and secretly. The group then discusses jobs that they all (in their assumed roles) could do together arriving at a specific number (5 or 10). Their last task is to choose the jobs from their list that they each could do best.

Variations:
1. Give children a list of tasks and have them select from among their group members the most qualified people to do each job.
2. Give each group member a suggestion for creating his/her role description, for example:

   a. An educated person
   b. A person who is very useful in a technological society
   c. A person considered a social outcast
   d. A versatile person
   e. A creative person

FOSSIL FUN

Objective: **To better understand causes and effects.**

Materials: Bones, ferns, leaves, nuts, and other similar natural materials as well as hardening clay.

Procedure: Make fossil replicas using the materials listed. Then, with groups of eight to ten children prepare a geological or archaeological "dig." Have the groups examine each other's findings and explain how the fossils came to be gathered at this site.

Variation: After studying a particular culture, its agricultural or land use patterns, its means of livelihood, its use of tools, have the children design their "dig" to reflect this cultures' distinctive way of life.

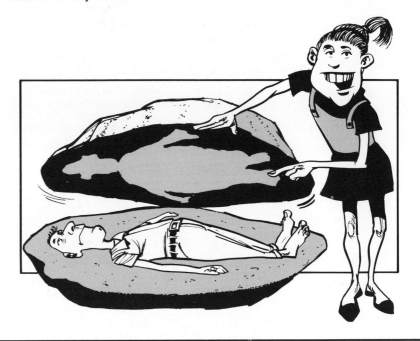

SCIENCE

Objective: **To help children realize their potential inventive abilities.**

Materials: Putty, popsicle sticks, pins, paper clips, work mats—for each child.

Procedure: Have the students either in groups or as individuals devise and construct on their work mats a balance or some other simple machine from the materials listed. After all have finished, have a demonstration of each product with an accompanying sales pitch. Many features can be added by increasing the variety of materials made available to the children or having them add one or more materials of their own. Have them make a chart of the special features and functions of the machine to use in their sales pitch. They may want to pretend that their invention is a model of a much larger machine.

Variation: Have children exchange "machines" before making up the sales pitch. The teacher or the class may decide whether or not to have these machines named and labeled before the exchange.

LET'S PRETEND

Objective: **To develop understanding that sounds convey mood and feeling.**

Procedure: Let the students pretend to be any size or kind of bell they would like. Tell them to simulate the sounds of that particular type of bell. They may also discuss the reasons for having so many different sounding bells and the various moods that these sounds create.

Variation: Have the children vary the tone and pitch of their voices while repeating the same word or phrase. For example, have them feign a high voice, a low voice, an excited voice.

FOLLOW ALONG GAME

Objective: **To develop a sense of the rhythmic qualities of language.**

Procedure: The children clap in rhythm. As they clap the teacher gives directions in rhythm. The child called upon responds on the next set of claps. *For example:* The teacher sets up a four-beat rhythm by clapping on the first and third beat.

```
        Number one now   give a verb (rest)
        clap      clap   clap      clap
         1  2  3   4       1  2  3   4
Child:
        Here's my verb rest   It is "walking"
        clap       clap   clap      clap
         1    2    3    4    1 2    3    4
```

Variation: Children may be asked to respond with words, numbers, or historical events.

RADIO ANNOUNCEMENT

Objective: To help children understand the purpose and function of public service announcements.

Materials: Tape recorder.

Procedure: Have children each simulate, using a tape recorder, a one-minute public service announcement urging people to do one of the following:

1. Eat more ostrich eggs.
2. Smile.
3. Vote.
4. Save energy in some particular way.
5. Exercise for health.
6. Protect unicorns.
7. Show brotherhood.
8. Promote peace among ant colonies.
9. Bring back King George to the throne of England; make the United States a British colony.

Discuss why television and radio stations make public service announcements. Do stations charge for them? Why would some of the suggested topics on the list never be broadcast by stations? How do stations decide which announcements to make for which groups of people?

Variation: Have the children pretend to be a television station manager who must decide which *one* public service announcement from the list needs to be made.

PING-PONG SPEECHES

Objective: To encourage improvisation.

Materials: Ping-Pong balls. seat students on floor

Procedure: Throw a Ping-Pong ball in the air. Whoever the ball touches first has to give a two-minute campaign speech for his favorite sports or entertainment figure as future governor of the state. He or she then throws the ball in the air again.

Variation: Alternate speeches in favor of the candidate with those opposed.

EYEWITNESSES

Objective: To help in recognizing the tremendous variation in people's perceptions and accounts of the same event.

Materials: Tape recorder and/or microphone.

Procedure: Have one child be the man or woman on-the-street television reporter and ask the other children to be eyewitnesses to dramatic historical events like:

1. The assassination of President Kennedy, President Lincoln, Martin Luther King
2. A famous battle such as Pearl Harbor, or Shiloh
3. Demonstrations of a famous invention such as the telephone, the printing press, the steamboat

Variations:
1. Use an event children have actually seen.
2. Use fantastic or imaginary events like the sudden sprouting of Jack's beanstalk, or a visit from Peter Pan and Tinkerbell.

LET'S COMMUNICATE

Objective: **To increase power of imaginative invention and visualization.**

Materials: "Pixie" toys.

Procedure: Bring an invisible "pixie" to class hidden in a pocket. Hold it up for the students to see. Then ask them to describe the pixie. Next hold him to your ear and tell the children that he wants to whisper something to a particular child. Act it out and then ask the child to explain the pixie's message. Finally, pretend that the pixie must leave. After it has gone have the children speculate about where the pixie went, about pixie homes, and pixie life. Afterwards show dolls and crafts that are supposed to represent pixies.

Variation: Use an invisible animal friend.

PET EMOTIONS

Objective: **To develop empathy with and understanding of animals.**

Materials: Pictures of pets and plants.

Procedure: Display pictures of pets and plants and talk about whether these feel angry, happy, sad, or scared. Make up situation questions for the children to answer.

Examples: When I go to school my pet hates to see me go because _____
I know my pet's favorite food because _____
My pet is frightened by _____
My pet's favorite game is _____

Variations:
1. Discuss how pets make children feel.
2. Have children discuss ways to make pets and plants happier and more content.

COLOR FUN

Objective: **To increase verbal descriptive abilities.**

Procedure: Have children try to simulate how they would describe the color red to a person who is blind and has never seen any color. They might choose any other color or the concept of darkness.

Variation: Have children attempt to describe something that is visually beautiful like a sunset, an artistic masterpiece, a scenic view, a famous monument or building.

THE BABY'S IMPRESSION

Objective: **To enhance abilities to see things from other viewpoints and perspectives.**

Procedure: Have the children pretend that they are babies less than one day old. Each child should describe his or her first impression of the world. They might want to talk about the thing that frightened them most, the reason they were happy to be alive, or what they were unhappiest about.

Variation: Have children pretend to be parents expressing their first reactions to the baby's arrival.

LANGUAGE FUN

Objective: To develop an awareness of and sensitivity to the many ways that people communicate.

Procedure: Have children in small groups act out their solutions to the following problem: "You have just arrived in a foreign country and cannot speak the language. Communicate (without words) to the people of that country, who you are, where you're from, and what you want." They might try to communicate a particular question such as:

1. How do I get to a particular town?
2. How do I find my hotel?
3. How could I buy some food?
4. Where is the nearest telephone? Police station? Person who speaks English?

Variation: Children might act out attempts to communicate with people who are deaf, blind, or very ill. This may lead to a discussion of international sign language.

JUNGLE LIFE

Objective: To develop an awareness of the impact that past experiences have on present attitudes, perceptions, and understanding.

Procedure: Ask children to pretend they were raised in the jungle and have never seen any other people. Have them express their first reactions to such modern sights as a super highway, a factory, a computer, an airplane, an animated cartoon, or a supermarket.

Variation: Ask the children to imagine themselves responsible for introducing these jungle people to modern American society and culture. Have them discuss and decide upon a group of things that these people *should* see and experience.

SPELLING WORD GUESS

Objective: To increase word association power through dramatic expression.

Materials: Weekly spelling list.

Procedure: Each child chooses a partner and they act out in pantomime selected spelling words. They may use meaning clues as well as syntactical and sound clues. As in the game of charades, a signal system may be developed for frequently used clues such as "sounds like," "part of speech," "dividing into syllables." This can serve as a fascinating and engrossing alternative to a spelling test or pretest.

Variation: Have the children each make up three to five sentences using the week's spelling words. They read their sentences orally, omitting the featured words that the rest of the class must then guess.

CHECKLIST OF IDEAS FOR CREATIVE DRAMATICS

1. **"Helping" role plays.** For primary children, pantomiming or role playing the many helping activities around the home are effective starters for creative dramatics (e.g., helping bake a cake, wash clothes, change the baby, fix the car, build a play house, train the puppy).

2. **Going visiting.** Personal visits and school field trips are good sources for pantomimes and role plays. Enact visits to the zoo, the circus, the rodeo, the railroad station, the airport, the amusement park (even special ones like Opryland or Disney World). Some children can portray visitors while others can be part of the sights and activities at the place visited.

3. **Personal encounters.** Children working in pairs can have enjoyable experiences role playing the following:
   a. Telephone conversations
   b. Taxicab drivers and passengers
   c. A father/mother teaching a daughter/son to drive, cook, bowl, ice skate
   d. A nurse and a difficult patient
   e. First date situations
   f. A fortuneteller and a patron
   g. A person rediscovering Aladdin's lamp, King Arthur's sword, the magic tinderbox
   h. A policeman questioning a witness
   i. Unlikely conversations between two or more famous people from different historical periods
   j. Animals' conversations about their owners

4. **Occupational role play.** Different occupations may be role played or pantomimed in various ways including:
   a. As a guessing game with each child acting out an occupation in turn
   b. As a mock-confrontation between two or more people in different occupations over which is the most fulfilling or satisfying
   c. As they would be encountered in a person's home (a day in the life of James or Jane Smith with all of the people that might visit them)

5. **The big event.** To enact a sports event some of the following suggestions may be helpful:
   a. Have the children play guess games in which they try to give accurate but not obvious clues to the event they are portraying
   b. Ask students to act out discussions between the promoters and the media

c. Have children try simulating the conversations and feelings of the participants before, after, and long after the event

d. Ask children to supply the commentary as it would be given by different personalities

e. Have them simulate different people's reactions to watching the event (a participant's wife or child, the next challenger, the sponsor, a "trapped" nonsports fan, a person ignorant of the sport with an avid enthusiast, an ex-umpire or official, a former pro player).

6. **Something for everyone.** Daily activities are excellent role play resources. Children can act out their thoughts as they are going to sleep at night, and during their morning routines, hobbies, and recreation after school. They can also enact their impressions of other people's activities (older children, parents, teachers, other adults).

7. **Emotions.** Feelings can be portrayed and explored in many ways including:

a. Showing the different ways of expressing reaction words like "oh, ah, but, yes, and no" in various situations like winning the grand prize in a contest, being turned down for a job, finding out someone else has been given your room, getting a new puppy, being disappointed (or surprised) about a present.

b. Saying the same sentences with varying degrees of emphasis and emotional impact.

c. Portraying the reactions of several famous people to the same situations.

d. Acting out different emotions (happiness, surprise, anger, sadness, excitement, fear) in various ways.

8. **Modes of travel.** Discussion-role-plays are activities in which talking about the "roles" has more importance than the acting out of the roles. Traveling lends itself to discussion-role-play activity. Children can identify with situations like these:

a. Deciding which means of transportation to use and which route to take

b. The trip that never seems to end

c. Getting ready to go

d. Remembering you needed to bring something after you are on your way

e. Finding things to do on a long trip

f. Traveling with unpleasant people, people you do not like, people who irritate you with some habit or mannerism

g. Wanting/needing to stop and not being able to do so

h. Traveling when tired, unhappy, frightened, excited, bored, crowded, uncomfortable

i. Being lost

j. Traveling when you do not want to do so.

Creative Movement

BODY TALK

Objective: To help in the realization that every movement communicates feeling.

Procedure: Tell the children to make their bodies show how they feel:

joy	terror
sorrow	excitement
wonder	concern or worry
enchantment	glee
despair	resentment
fear	anger

Variation: Have the children move different parts of their bodies in particular ways for each feeling. For example, how could they walk, nod their heads, or wave their hands to express anger, sorrow, or fear?

LEGS

Objective: To develop ability to move according to a prescribed pattern.

Materials: Blank sheets of paper, pens, sheets of paper with words on them.

Procedure: Tell children to draw a pattern on a piece of paper. Then have them walk (run, skip, jump, hop) that pattern (or let the children walk the pattern first and then draw it). Tell the children to walk the pattern of the letter that begins their first name. Then ask them:

What words can you spell through movement?
Walk the pattern of the word "walk."
Run the pattern of the word "run."
Skip the pattern of the word "skip."
Hop the pattern of the word "hop."

Have words already written out on paper.

Variation: Move in patterns that will form geometric shapes or more complicated letters like "x" and "z."

LOCOMOTION

Objective: To develop a greater sensitivity to location in movement.

Procedure: Have the children notice where they are standing. Tell them to move away from their home spot and then return when the signal *home* is called. Repeat this several times. Then tell them to look at a spot away from home and go to that spot as quickly as possible. Return them home. Tell them to find two spots away from home, visit one spot, then the other, and return home. Tell the children to move away from home in a "low" position (crouching, crawling) when the signal is given. Tell them to come home in another low position. Use a specific gesture to signal them to move from here to there in several different high (skipping, hopping) or low positions.

Variation: Give children various colors of tape. Have them mark their own home in a unique way.

POUNDING IT OUT

Objective: **To develop inventiveness in body expression.**

Procedure: Have children pretend they are something that "pounds," and show the pounding through body movement. (Variations include throbbing, thudding, scraping.) After a trial effort discuss the things they have done. Encourage children to use their entire bodies, not just arms and legs. Brainstorm about other things that pound and then have the children try several of the new ideas.

Variation: Have children pretend to be the "thing" being pounded.

RAG DOLLS

Objective: **To relax and loosen movement in order to express feelings better.**

Materials: A small, limp rag doll; a recording of slow, quiet music.

Procedure: Tell children to sit on the floor. Hold the rag doll with both hands and show the children how limp it is. Shake the doll and tell the children to look at the way its head and arms move. Have the children shake their heads and bodies and let them hang limp. Do the same for hands and arms. Play the record and have the children move like rag dolls. Have the children lie down as you go around to each one lifting their arms and legs gently. Let them drop saying, "Feel like a rag doll. Make your arms and legs feel heavy and floppy."

Variation: Have children pretend to be other types of toys such as marionettes, hand puppets, toy soldiers, teddy bears, bride dolls.

✦ SHAPING UP

Objective: To encourage a variety of stances and positions in movement.

Procedure: Tell the children to make themselves into shapes with each of the following characteristics:

1. Long and thin
2. Round and smooth
3. Prickly
4. Pointed
5. Flat or wide

6. Small and round
7. Many cornered
8. Oval or egglike
9. Wavy
10. Triangular

Be especially careful of personal sensitivity about height or weight.

Variation: Have the children assume a particular shape to express or represent an abstract concept (law, love, truth, hate, government, friend, enemy, liar).

PUSH BUTTONS

Objective: To develop physical expression of perceptions and concepts.

Materials: Circular "push buttons" cut out of sticky-backed paper.

Procedure: Stick a push button on each child and have him choose a machine to be (toaster, washing machine, electric saw). Tell another student to push someone's button and watch as the machine comes to life.

Variation: Have each child pretend to be a *small* part of a familiar machine repeating a single action over and over again. Have the other children try to guess what action is being represented.

STOPLIGHT

Objective: To develop ability to communicate ideas nonverbally.

Procedure: Let one child pretend to be a traffic signal and the other children the traffic at a four-way intersection. The child must figure out some way of conveying which light is green, which is red, and which is yellow.

Variation: Have each child attempt to portray a traffic sign (curve, no parking, road narrows, dead end).

SPRINGTIME FLOWERS

Objective: To develop imaginative expression and interpretive observation.

Procedure: Let the children pretend to be flowers that are beginning to bloom in the spring. Then have them guess the name of each other's flower.

Variation: Repeat the guessing game having the children portray various kinds of food being served at dinner.

THE STRANGE CREATURE

Objective: **To develop cohesive group expression of imaginative ideas.**

Procedure: Tell the children about a buffernuffertop, an animal with six legs, six arms, and three heads. Divide the children into groups of three and while holding on to each other in some manner have them imitate a buffernuffertop walking, running, dancing, eating, or laying down. Then have each group make up an alternative name for their creature. The teacher might suggest:

    a. words with three repetitions of syllables and letters (Boploplopeeetttooo)

    b. words with three successive rhyming syllables (crockrocksock)

    c. words that combine the names of three animals (Lionzebrasquirrel)

    d. terms that combine the numerical prefixes *tri-* or *sex-* with the name of some familiar animal suggestive of the creature's characteristics (the triturtle or sexipotamus).

    e. nonsense words

Variation: Have each child make this multilimbed, multiheaded creature using paper bags, cardboard tubes, tin cans, and other materials.

 MOVING SONGS

Objective: **To develop the ability to interpret song lyrics through creative movement.**

Procedure: Have the children express through creative movement each of the verses in cumulative songs ("Old MacDonald," "The Twelve Days of Christmas"). Pantomime motions can also be added to many of the familiar rounds ("Are you Sleeping," "Row, Row, Row Your Boat"), and narrative songs ("The Erie Canal," "Frankie and Johnnie," "Big John").

Variation: Do choral reading of poetry using movement to accompany each line of poetry. Eventually the shorter poems can be memorized and the motions synchronized with the reading, or the group may be divided in half with one part reading and the other moving.

THE MAGIC GARDEN

Objective: **To promote imaginative interpretation of natural growing processes.**

Procedure: Have each child think of things that grow in a garden. Then discuss "magic" things that grow in gardens and things that grow magically. The children must not tell anyone what they are thinking. While working in pairs have one child pretend to be the plant and the other the magic farmer. As the magic farmer plants his seed, the other child must demonstrate (by moving on the floor) what he or she represents in the garden. The magic farmer waters, hoes, and weeds the garden and the plant grows and bears leaves, fruit, or nuts.

Variations: 1. Change the garden location to an underwater garden or a garden in the clouds.

    2. Assign the garden a special purpose such as making people sleepy, happy, or angry.

 **A DIFFERENT DRUMMER**

Objective: **To develop the ability to move according to directions and to perceive the relationship between mood and movement.**

Materials: Any type of drum or percussion instrument (even a piano). Child-made drums, or beaters are especially nice.

Procedure: Tell the children that when you hit the drum, it means that you want them to stop what they are doing. Tell them that you want to watch how they walk. Each time the drum is struck have them change something about their walk either in response to such directions as these:

Show me how slowly you can walk.
Show me how fast you can walk.
See how close you can walk next to someone without touching them.
Take giant steps while you walk. Take small steps.
Walk using lots of space. Walk using a little bit of space.

or to such questions as the following:

How can you walk and make noise with your feet?
Can you walk and turn in a different direction when the drum is beaten twice?
How would you walk if you were going to the toy store? How would you walk if you were going some place you did not want to go?

Variation: Have children move to the different cadences, rhythms, and tones of varying instruments.

BODY NUMBERS

Objective: **To develop mathematical concepts through movement.**

Procedure: Let the children use their bodies in groups to demonstrate the math concepts "greater than" and "less than." For example: Choose one group of five children and another group of seven children. The group of five tries to show through movement that it is less than the group of seven. Conversely, the group of seven demonstrates that it is greater than the group of five.

Variations: 1. Have groups express other mathematical processes and concepts such as addition and subtraction of whole numbers, minus and plus, part of a set, etc.
2. Have the children try to represent with their bodies various whole numbers and fractions.

BODY IN ACTION

Objective: **To encourage listening through active participation.**

Materials: Musical recordings in varying moods and tempos, recordings of narrated stories, and finger puppets (may be made by children from construction paper).

Procedure: Have children sit in a circle, listen to a recording, and demonstrate how their finger puppets can dance to the music. For stories, each child (or pair of children) should have a puppet for each character. They let their puppets act out the story as it is told.

Variation: Let the fingers be other small objects that move (such as exploding firecrackers, crawling worms, caterpillars, the tongues of various animals).

PHYSICAL CONTACT

Objective: To increase realization that movement is used to express feelings as well as words.

Procedure: Have the children, by means of physical movement, respond to words that describe emotions (fear, sadness, anger, wonder).

Variations:
1. Use only hands to respond to the words.
2. Use only facial expression to respond to the words.
3. Read emotional passages from stories and have the children interpret each character's feelings.

DO I KNOW YOU?

Objective: To interpret emotional reactions through creative movement.

Procedure: Suggest situations involving a meeting between two people and ask the students to demonstrate varying emotional responses (for example, a meeting with an old friend or with someone you *think* you know but are not sure). Have the children react with their bodies, without using words, to illustrate the situation.

Variation: Portray each of the meeting situations as it might be handled by particular personality types such as:

1. Timid, shy people
2. Boisterous, loud people
3. Eager, excited people
4. Self-confident people
5. Fearful, worried people
6. Angry, rude people

CLASSROOM OBJECTS

Objective: To develop expressive movement as a method of description.

Materials: Objects found regularly in the classroom (chalk, desk, book).

Procedure: Have the students create a series of movements to explain the use of some object. They demonstrate without words how the object functions.

Variation: While keeping time to music, have the children use a classroom object as a prop, simply moving with it, focusing attention on it.

music?.

ADD A MOVEMENT

Objective: To develop muscle coordination in response to music.

Materials: Songs, records, radio.

Procedure: Have the children move their bodies in a consistent, repetitious manner in response to music. With every phrase, measure, or line played, a new motion must be added to the previous movements (for example; line one—nod head; line two—nod head, stamp foot; line three—nod head, stamp foot, wave hand).

Variation: Limit movements to a particular type such as birdlike movements, or exercise movements.

DRUMBEAT

Objective: **To relate rhythmic response to creative movement.**

Materials: Drum, drumstick.

Procedure: To the count of eight drumbeats, have the children react to words called out by the teacher. When the teacher calls out a new word, the children immediately change their responses. Interesting words might include: lion, witch, ghost, fiddlebug, crab, disco, church.

Variation: Blink a light in rhythm instead of beating a drum. Have the children move in a circle and change direction with each new word.

HOMEWORK

Objective: **To develop powers of descriptive suggestion through movement.**

Materials: Direction cards, props for household chores.

Procedure: Give out secret direction cards that tell children to act out the following tasks.

1. Washing dishes
2. Doing laundry
3. Mowing the lawn
4. Painting a house
5. Shingling a roof
6. Fixing a leaky pipe
7. Weeding the garden
8. Making a bed
9. Washing windows
10. Raking leaves
11. Taking out the garbage
12. Putting groceries away
13. Shoveling snow
14. Ironing
15. Putting in electric wiring

When children are called on they must choose a prop inappropriate for their chore. Then they act out the assigned chore using the wrong prop but conveying the right message.

Variation: Have the children demonstrate each task as it might be performed by several different persons, for example: an old person, a clown, a "cool" teenager, or an accident-prone person.

HISTORY ON THE MOVE

Objective: **To develop the ability to interpret musical mood through movement.**

Procedure: Have children think of a popular song title to describe a historical event. Then have them dramatize the event with humorous and exaggerated motions while the song is being played, hummed, or whistled.

Variation: Have children carry on a conversation by singing songs. The first group sings a phrase or line from one song and a second group responds with a line from another song. This may be planned out in advance or played as a game with timed responses. (Songbooks can be very helpful.) For example one group can portray a tramp trying to get a free room and the other his intended host.

Group 1 (sings) "All I want is a room somewhere."
Group 2 (sings) "There's a small hotel"
Group 1 (sings) "I got plenty of nothin'."
Group 2 (sings) "Who's sorry now."

HANDS AND FEET

Objective: **To utilize movement as a learning medium to increase sensitivity about the feelings of others.**

Procedure: Tell the children: "Look at your feet and pretend they are the feet of Methuselah. Make you feet old. Move them as though they were old; take a few minutes to explore this feeling." Then ask them if their old feet made the rest of their bodies (their hands, their ears) feel differently. Now ask them to look at their hands. "Watch them grow greedy and grasping like the hands of Scrooge. Count your money." Explore the effects of this movement by asking the children how this makes them feel.

Variation: Use the physical features of other literary characters such as Captain Ahab's harpoon arm, Wilbur's (of *Charlotte's Web*) tail, or Mary Poppin's eyes.

INFLUENCE OF GROUP

Objective: **To gain awareness through movement of the influence of groups on individual behavior.**

Procedure: Divide the class into small groups and have them move as the class influences them to move . . . never touching one another. Do not worry too much if nothing occurs immediately. Wait for the children to respond and offer minimum guidance. If children stand around too long have them close their eyes and begin swaying. If nothing happens give them clues like: Do you feel people are getting too close or too far away? Do you feel as though people near you like you? Do you feel tension in the group?

Variation: Have an individual child or small group try to influence the class's feelings and movements through thought direction (concentrating on a single purpose with such force that others will sense it) or modeling (doing something in such a way that others will imitate the action). In neither case should any verbal direction be given.

Manipulatory Activities

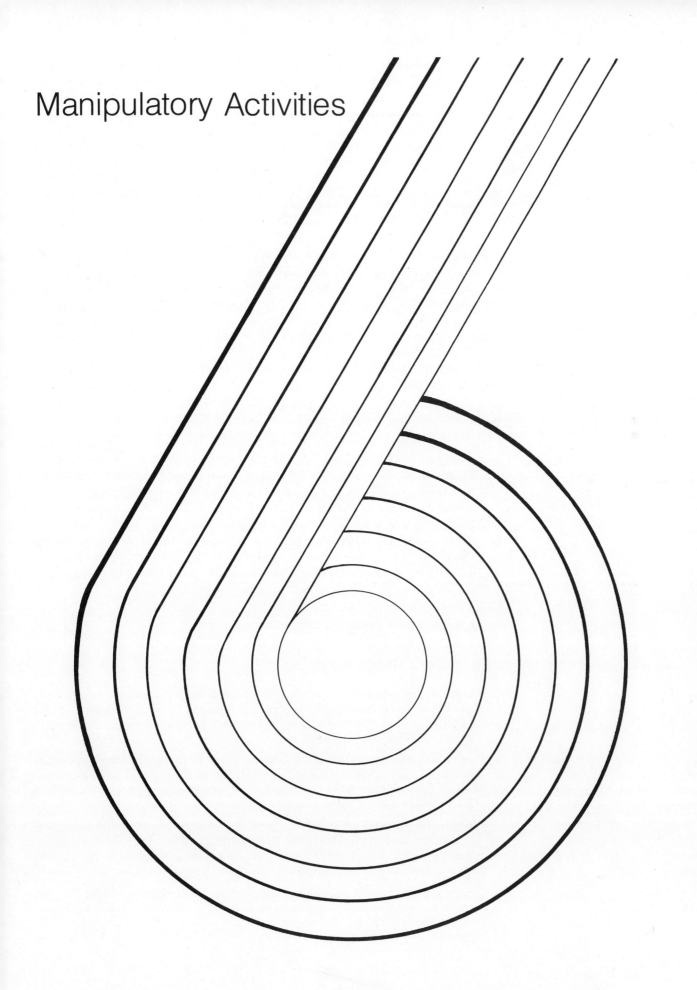

Manipulation has been selected for this chapter's title because the term brings together many different activities. It characterizes a variety of forms of creative expression, all of which basically involve doing things with the hands. Manipulation necessarily implies an object, something being manipulated and is characteristic of those activities which involve the children in crafts, art, experimentation, or anything else in which he or she tries to actually effect change in the physical world. Manipulatory activities provide the child with the most observable and tangible results of all creative forms. There are almost always products. Something is changed and the change can be seen by both the creator and others. The child has a visible monument to his or her creativity.

Children encounter many and varied opportunities through manipulation activities. They can explore and discover the feel of things, how things react to change, the sensory affects of things, and a host of other sensory and experiential phenomena. They can give their concepts and perceptions physical reality, thus making the studies of other cultures and times, of abstract concepts, and of feelings have concrete reality. They can transform trash into art and a blank page into a feast of ideas and beauty. Manipulatory activities can provide ways of solving problems, choosing solutions, and envisioning ideas which are too abstract, too complex, or too large to control in word and thought alone.

MAINSPRINGS OF SUCCESSFUL MANIPULATORY ACTIVITIES

1. Establish safety rules appropriate to grade level and individual group makeup. Inform and remind children of these often, and *enforce* them.
2. Ensure all needed materials are on hand and in control *before* beginning.
3. Allow time to clean up, and *prevent* cleanup problems by advance preparation.
4. Allow sufficient time for the planned activities.
5. Ensure there are adequate facilities for storing incomplete and fragile things.
6. Provide for personal clean up and protection of children's clothing.
7. Display the work of every child and comment on it.
8. Invite parental help and participation.
9. Be open to new ideas and suggestions.

MESS MAKER MASTERPIECES—SOME FAR-OUT IDEAS

1. **Sawdust pictures.** Soak sawdust in colored diluted tempera paint. Then place sawdust on newspaper to dry. The colored sawdust can be used for sculpturing or it may be applied to areas which have been spread with glue to make unusual pictures.

2. **Crayon and tempera.** Use crayons to draw a design on black construction paper and cover with diluted white tempera paint. The crayon-covered surface will not absorb the paint. This produces an interesting effect. (Other colors can be used also.)

3. **Vegetable printing.** Use carrots, potatoes, or turnips cut in a cross section. Cut designs into the flat sections. Use a paint brush to cover the design with tempera paint. Press on cloth, paper, or pastel construction paper. The varying material and vegetable textures will produce different effects.

4. **Crayon pictures.** Sketch or block in areas with brightly colored crayons on paper. Cover with black crayon and scratch through with a sharp object or fingernail to sketch a design.

5. **Sponge paintings.** Use sponges cut in one inch or larger squares instead of brushes to paint with tempera.

6. **Sand and coffee grounds.** Add sand or coffee grounds and glue to tempera paint to make a textured paint.

7. **Colored chalk on sandpaper.** Draw designs or pictures with the chalk on sandpaper. Try burlap and other textured cloth as well.

8. **Detergent snow.** Mix one-half cup of detergent with water in a cup until the mixture assumes the consistency of whipped cream. Apply with a tongue depressor. This produces a snowlike effect useful in decorating activities.

9. **Stone sculpture.** Use various sizes and shapes of stones. Paint the stones or select stones of contrasting colors and textures. Cover a flat board. Use the stones to form a mosaic picture.

10. **Wax carvings.** Melt wax in containers and add broken pieces of crayon. Pour the wax mixture into a milk carton and let it stand until hard. Tear away the milk carton and carve the wax.

11. **Box aquarium.** Cut large windows in the sides of a box. Paste blue and green cellophane on the inside to cover the windows. Arrange construction paper, stones, moss, and sand inside the box to resemble the ocean bottom. Color and cut fish and attach them to a thread fastened at the top of the box. Close and seal the top of the box. Paint the outside if desired.

12. **Branch mobiles.** Have children collect interesting tree branches or weathered pieces of wood. Spray the branches with paint. Cut out and color various shapes and forms from construction paper. Punch a hole in the top of each paper cutout and hang it from a branch with string.

13. **Collages.** Collect junk (odds and ends) and keep it stored in various boxes. Collect materials that have different textures such as smooth, rough, scratchy, sandy, fluffy and crinkly. Children glue things from the boxes onto paper to make collages and murals.

14. **Soap flake pictures.** Mix wet tempera paint with soap flakes. Use this substance to paint textured pictures.

15. **Nuts and bolts.** Dip bolts, nuts, corks, or spools into tempera paint to make designs.

16. **Wet chalk painting.** With a paper towel wet a sheet of darkly colored construction paper. While wet, use brightly colored chalk to draw picture designs. Let the picture dry and "fix" with hair spray.

17. **Seeing perspectives.** Fold papers in halves or quarters. Draw a simple still life from different perspectives (top, bottom, sides). Use one section of the paper to show each perspective.

18. **Wax paper resist.** Cover a piece of white construction paper with a sheet of wax paper. On the wax paper scratch a design with a blunt instrument (end of a paint brush). Then cover the entire sheet of construction paper with a thin watercolor wash. The wax from the wax paper will resist the watercolor and the design will stand out.

19. **Mood art.** Listen to a musical composition. Have students make a rhythmic pattern out of clay, wood, and string. Then paint it.

20. **Wild thing.** After introducing *Where the Wild Things Are* by Maurice Sendak, let the students create a "wild thing" using egg cartons, colored tissues, wool, balls of crushed newspaper, cardboard boxes or tubes.

21. **Face to face.** Each student is given a pair of scissors and a piece of construction paper. He is to cut out his impression of how his face looks.

22. **Stained glass windows.** Draw a simple line design on a sheet of black construction paper. Cut out some of the spaces between the lines. Clip this sheet to another of the same size. Fold a large piece of wax paper in half (it should measure the same as the black paper when folded). Tear or cut colored tissue paper designs. Put the tissue paper between the folded sheets of wax paper. Place the designed wax paper between the black frames and fasten together. Display them near or in a window.

23. **Confetti or stained glass.** Sketch a stained glass window design using white pencil on black paper. Paint each section of the design with glue and while it is still wet sprinkle confetti, glitter, colored sand, or sequins over the glued area. Finish filling in all the necessary spaces with one color before starting another.

24. **Torn paper mosaics.** Tear various colors of paper into approximately ½-inch pieces. Glue pieces to a single contrasting sheet of colored paper to make a mosaiclike picture.

PUPPETS CHILDREN CAN MAKE

FINGER PUPPETS

1. Paper or lightweight cardboard (index card) loops fitted to the end of the fingers are the basis for many types of finger puppets. The head or entire body of the desired character can be drawn on precut strips of cardboard or stiff paper. Each strip is then attached to a loop. (Staples are not recommended. However, if staples are used be sure to face points outward from the center.)

2. Small pictures from postcards, brochures, old books, or magazines can be cut out and glued or taped to the cardboard loop.

3. Puppet characters can be drawn directly on the fingers using *washable* felt-tip markers. (Assure access to plenty of soap and water.)

4. The fingers may be cut from old gloves and rubber gloves. Figures can be attached to the fingers or drawn directly on them. With the rubber glove one character can be washed off and another drawn on.

5. The "round people" puppets can be made from damaged Ping Pong balls. Cut a hole in the ball and draw on a face.

6. Large, deep bottle lids can be painted and decorated with glued-on figures to form finger puppets.

7. Many commercial finger puppets and toy "people" can be used as they are or redecorated with color, "makeup," costume, and hair.

8. One-inch diameter short pieces of dowel (or square one-by-one-inch lumber) can be turned into finger puppets. A hole ½-inch in diameter and about ½-to¾-inch deep should be predrilled by an adult.

9. Mold clay around a small hollow cardboard tube or directly to the finger to make animal and people finger puppets.

10. Small cardboard tubes (such as those on which wide gauge bandage rolls come) can become interesting tall finger puppets.

STICK PUPPETS

1. Paint or draw faces on ice cream sticks and tongue depressors.

2. Draw faces on pieces of lightweight cardboard or construction paper. Glue or staple them to the cardboard tubes found on clothes hangers.

3. Brooms, mops, shovels, rakes, and other long-handled tools can be turned quite easily into large-as-life attractive and amusing stick puppets. The "business" end becomes the head of the puppet and the handle becomes the body. Use construction paper, cloth scraps, rope and colored yarn to make facial features and clothing. Large cartoonlike eyes made from two layers of contrasting colored paper add to the puppet's caricature quality.

4. Both types of wooden clothespins can be used to make storytelling puppets. Clothesline can be strung across the room or across a puppet stage and the clothespin puppets can easily be attached and removed. Draw faces on the clothespins with fine-tip felt markers or make paper faces and staple, paste, or glue these to the clothespins. (The flat surface of the spring clip type clothespin makes these work better for glueing.)

BOX PUPPETS

1. Cover single serving size milk cartons with construction paper and cut a mouth in the middle. Remove the bottom or cut hand holds in the back of the carton to make the puppet's mouth move.

2. Single serving size cereal boxes may be cut and folded in reverse to make a "bill" mouth.

3. Wrap a large box as a gift. Cut across the top of the box and down along two sides. The uncut bottom forms a hinge. This produces a mouthlike opening that can be moved up and down. Make hand holes on the back or attach a string to the upper part of the box to open and close the mouth. Eyes can be added for effect.

4. Oatmeal boxes

5. Shoe box lids lift to represent the opening of a puppet's mouth.

CLOTH-BODY PUPPETS

Things to use as heads:

1. old tennis balls—cut a hole in the ball big enough for the index finger.

2. round-shaped vegetables and fruits such as potatoes, apples, bell peppers—avoid squishy vegetables like tomatoes.

3. clay

4. a mixture of sawdust and glue—this can be molded.

5. Papier-mâché—use a cardboard, paper, or Ping Pong ball core.

6. carved balsa wood

7. small balloons—only slightly inflated.

8. serving size cereal boxes

9. four ounce size margarine containers—make a hole for the child's finger but keep the lid on.

10. cardboard tubes from bathroom tissue, paper towels and snack foods.

11. small food and juice cans

12. old doll heads

ALL-CLOTH PUPPETS

1. Use a rag doll or cut stuffed animal patterns a little wider at the bottom and do not sew the bottoms together.

2. Make distinctive sock puppets using yarn hair, old jewelry, felt, sequins, or buttons for the eyes and nose. Make bill mouths from the two halves of a broken tongue depressor. For a stiffer mouth glue on pieces of cardboard or light wood.

3. Turn a small pillow into a spider puppet by attaching yarn or braided yarn for legs and an elastic string to move it up and down. By the same procedure a small bolster type pillow can become an insect or worm.

4. Gloves and mittens can be turned into multieyed, multiarmed or multilegged creature puppets. These can be very expressive.

5. Oven mittens (insulated glove-type potholders) can be easily transformed into snake and lizard puppets.

6. The sleeves of old shirts, dresses, and robes can be cut off and sewn together at one end to make interesting puppets.

7. Large-picture, preschool coloring books and picture books can be used to make puppet patterns by cutting duplicate pieces of the desired picture, sewing them together around the edges, and then turning them inside out. For this purpose a soft material with little nap or texture is preferable. It sews more easily and the facial features can be traced or drawn with a variety of materials. If desired these puppets can also be stuffed.

MASKS CHILDREN CAN MAKE

BENT CLOTHES HANGER MASKS

Bend a wire coat hanger so that the opening is wider than the child's face and the hook is at the bottom. An old nylon stocking is then forced over the coat hanger from the top. The resulting gauzelike mask will be taut, semitransparent, and will distort the features when held against the face. This mask can be decorated with felt-tip markers or simply left plain.

PAPER BAG MASKS

Paper bags slightly larger than children's heads are needed. Draw faces on the bags, cut them out of magazines, or make them using construction paper, yarn, etc. As an interesting variation create a collage mask which illustrates an "idea" about the person.

STICK MASKS

Draw a face larger than the child's on lightweight cardboard and then cut it out. A stick handle (cardboard tubing from a hanger, a thin short wood slat) is glued, stapled, or taped to the cardboard. One child can use two or more of these, changing characters or emotions through his or her mask. (These may also be made from a cardboard fan).

PAPIER-MÂCHÉ MASKS

For papier-mâché masks it is first necessary to have a solid "head shape" to work on. Several types of frames are possible; (1) inflated balloons that are burst after the mask has been built; (2) head size cardboard boxes; (3) crossed strips of cardboard stood on edge and notched together. Three to seven layers of paper are usually needed. The mask should be allowed to dry thoroughly before painting. The frame should be removed *after* painting.

ICE CREAM CARTON MASKS

Large commercial (3 gallon) ice cream containers make excellent mask material. These can be obtained free from most places where hand-packed ice cream and ice cream cones are sold. It is usually a good idea to first paint the containers and let them dry. The children can decorate them cutting out holes for the eyes and mouth, and glueing on hair and features. The masks can be made to resemble Indian masks, totem poles, clown masks, and space monsters.

MAGAZINE COVER MASKS

The child finds a large picture of a face on a magazine cover (or inside). The picture is pasted to a piece of lightweight cardboard and carefully cut out. Leave a wide border or at least enough of a margin to punch holes for string.

BODY MASKS

Pillow cases and large paper or cloth shopping bags can be used to make "masks" for the upper part of the body. Decorate them with felt-tip markers or crayons, or sew on features.

NAME GAME

Objective: To develop hand-eye coordination and flexibility in thinking.

Materials: Construction paper, pencils, scissors, glue.

Procedure: Have children write their names in cursive in large wide letters on the fold of a piece of paper. Then have them cut out their name. Make sure that they do not try to cut out the inside of open letters and that they keep all the letters attached, not cutting any of them apart. Next have them glue the newly formed figure on a different colored piece of construction paper. If they cut out the name in several thicknesses of paper, they can position the various pieces upside down, sideways, or backwards. Have the children invent a name for each of the figures, perhaps one associated with their own personality, perhaps a nonsensical name.

Variations:
1. Let children mix up the shapes and try to guess the names.
2. Allow children to search for interesting words to cut out.

A PORTRAIT OF TIME

Objective: To develop greater understanding of historical concepts.

Materials: Paper, pencils, crayons, paint and brush, colored chalk. Prints of impressionistic, surrealistic, and other modern art forms.

Procedure: Tell the students to draw and paint their own impressions of a historical movement or period. Ask them to draw or paint, for example, the settlers of Jamestown arriving in 1607 or the American Rebellion. To help the children select a topic, perhaps a list of interesting historical events might be provided or the works of modern artists displayed. Encourage the children to try capturing or representing the ideas and feelings behind the events. Have them also try to guess what event each painting depicts.

Variation: Have children mold in clay a "spirit of —-" statue for a particular event in history.

SANDBOX SURVIVAL

Objective: To develop the realization that environment is essential for survival.

Materials: A sandbox or sand table, plants, rocks, clay, and other natural materials.

Procedure: In a sandbox let children create a natural environment that distinguishes land-mass formations and soil types, and that shows water distribution, animal and plant life. Additional environmental information (climatic conditions for example) can be displayed on a piece of posterboard and hung from the ceiling above the sandbox. Ask the children to pretend they are stranded in this geographical region and in order to survive they must find a source of water, food provisions, and adequate shelter.

Variation: Using a sand table, have children make simplified topographical maps. Ask them to decide on the best locations for roads, housing communities, and cities. As a follow-up activity the children could construct a model housing structure or road-way from the available materials.

WILL IT FLOAT?

Objective: To explore buoyancy in water.

Materials: Bucket of water, variety of objects that either float or do not float in water.

Procedure: Without placing the objects in water, ask the children to decide which will float and which will not. After all the objects are separated into float and nonfloat categories, have the children try each object. A new category, "floats for a while," might need to be added. Children can experiment, combining items to make them float or sink.

Variations:
1. Pick a single object and have children determine which of the other objects are heavier and which are lighter without lifting them.
2. Have children predict which of several objects rolled down an inclined plane will go the farthest. Make a list of these showing the relative distance each moved.

SURFACE AREA

Objective: **To develop inventive measurement methods.**

Materials: Ball of string, hollow rubber balls, scissors, tape measure, rulers and meter sticks.

Procedure: Have children try to measure the surface area of the ball. They may cut the ball in any way, use any object or measuring device. (Clue: one method winds the string around the ball and measures the string.) See how many accurate ways of measuring they can devise.

Variation: Have children find ways of measuring straws and tin cans, the surface areas of irregularly shaped objects, the heights of buildings and trees, the weights of vegetables, or quantities of liquid.

ROCKS

Objective: **To develop classification skills.**

Materials: Rocks of varying shapes, sizes, textures that children find themselves.

Procedure: Each child finds at least five different ways to group the rocks and shares this information with the class.

Variation: Have the children catagorize buttons, paintings, words, games, or objects in the classroom into groups.

SEE VIEW

Objective: To develop sequencing skills and improve sequence classification concepts.

Materials: A large cardboard box, two dowel sticks or broomsticks (each longer than the box is wide), either a roll of shelf paper or tape to fasten sheets of school paper together, a variety of pictures, paste, glue, crayons or paints.

Procedure: Cut a hole as a viewing screen in front of the box. Make the screen slightly narrower than the width of the paper. Cut two holes on each side of the box to insert the sticks through. Holes should be exactly opposite to each other and one should be above the screen and one below it. The roll of paper is placed on one stick and the end of the paper attached to the other. The various pictures are pasted or drawn on the paper keeping a "unit" width equal to the screen's height. The pictures are then rolled through in sequence. Children can write a story for a set of pictures, make up the picture sequence to go with a given story, illustrate a series of ideas, or combine language experience stories. They can pretend the box is a television, a magic mirror, or a story box.

Variations:
1. Have children make tape recordings to accompany various films.
2. Use wide (30-inch or 36-inch) paper to make wide screen series.
3. Have children with good eye-hand coordination experiment with making drawn film strips or slides. Old film strips and slides can be cleaned with bleach. Special felt-tip markers and paints as well as blank tapes can be purchased from several companies.

THE GREAT KITE EXPOSITION

Objective: To explore and discover basic principles of flight.

Materials: Tissue paper, wooden strips, string, rags, paint, brushes. Pictures of oriental kites, box kites, etc.

Procedure: Talk about and show pictures of different kites. Have each student design and make a kite other than the standard flat diamond shape. Let them fly their kites outside. The question to explore is, "Why do some fly while others do not?" Explore such related issues as the importance of the tail on the kite, the solution to weight and balance problems, ways of initiating takeoffs, and feeding out string. Have a kite display, a kite flying contest, or kite fights.

Variation: Have children design kites depicting concepts or facts studied in particular subjects (metric kites, tall-tale kites, medieval kites, Chinese kites).

SPIDER AND WEB

Objective: **To develop adaptation as a creative skill.**

Materials: Construction paper, pipe cleaners, yarn, tape. Pictures of various spiders and other insects.

Procedure: Have each child create a spider out of the paper and pipe cleaners. Then on the wall, take the yarn and make a large web and have each child place his spider in the web. Discuss the good that spiders do and the stories in which spiders appear (*Charlotte's Web, Robert Bruce and the Spider*).

Variation: Let children make other insects, or caterpillars and worms and place them on a tree or on bulletin boards.

WEIGH-IN

Objective: **To develop variable techniques for measuring weight.**

Materials: Scales (balance type), variety of objects.

Procedure: Tell the children they are going to classify the objects according to weight. They may weigh the objects anyway they wish except by placing them directly on the scales.

Variation: Have each child choose a standard unit of weight to which they compare all other objects. If their unit is marbles, for example, a tablet of paper might weigh 20 marbles.

HIDDEN PICTURES

Objective: **To increase perceptiveness.**

Materials: Paper, pencil or crayons.

Procedure: Have children close their eyes and draw freely with a large crayon on newsprint. Then have them look for a hidden picture to color and develop.

Variation: Have children draw only straight lines or curved lines.

CLOCKWORK

Objective: **To increase awareness of time periods.**

Procedure: Tell the children to pretend they are clocks at different times of the day. After showing the time of the day, tell them to act out what a clock princess, or a clock dragon or a clock frog might do at that time. Having them design a "clock costume" out of tagboard or lightweight cardboard enhances the illusion.

Variation: Have children estimate the number of seconds it will take them to do certain short tasks. Or have them estimate the minutes they regularly spend engaged in particular activities.

THE CHANGING SCARF

Objective: **To develop flexibility, and originality in thinking.**

Materials: Several long scarves.

Procedure: Give each child a scarf and ask them how many things they can make. Encourage the children to use their imaginations, perhaps to think of themselves as some favorite animals, storybook or television characters. A stick or a ball can be very helpful in this activity.

Variation: Have children use hats, tissue paper, canes, balls, or the like in the same way.

TIME CAPSULE

Objective: **To develop a better concept of changing lifestyles.**

Procedure: Select items for a time capsule to represent the way we live and the major events of our day. Make up a time capsule for several different periods in history. If the children do not have a needed item they must make a facsimile.

Variation: Have children decide what items to send in a space capsule to the people on a different planet.

PROBLEMS

Objective: **To increase question-asking skill and encourage curiosity.**

Materials: Paper, pencils.

Procedure: Give students the names of common objects (tree, hammer, wind, tin can). Ask them to write down problems that they associate with each object. For example, given the word "candle," the following problems emerge:

1. How to light it?
2. Keeping it from falling over
3. Keeping it burning steadily
4. How long will it burn?
5. What to do with the drippings?

The problems should deal with the object's use, its shape and substance. Don't waste time thinking of ways to get the objects or to dispose of them.

Variation: Place questions on separate pieces of paper in a box. These questions give clues to a mystery object. Each child in turn draws out a clue question until the object is identified. Then the children try to guess what clues remain.

CARTOONS

Objective: **To develop ability to envision ideas represented by words.**

Materials: A box containing various cartoons or cartoon captions, paper, pencils, crayons.

Procedure: Have each child draw a caption from the box and then illustrate it, or reverse the procedure and choose a cartoon and write a caption.

Variation: Combine the illustrations to make a mural.

ROAD SIGNS

Objective: **To increase awareness of the purposes of road signs.**

Materials: Paper, pencil, scissors, cardboard.

Procedure: The teacher leads a discussion about road signs, "What do they mean?" "Are they satisfactory?" "Do they communicate the meaning visually without words?" "Could they be improved?" Next have each student design a set of road signs for a city of the future.

Variation: Have students design road signs for a barnyard, for a zoo, for a city without cars or trucks, and for a city of the past.

CONNECT THE DOTS

Objective: **To develop perceptual skills in identifying configurations.**

Materials: Connect-the-dot puzzle, pencils, paper.

Procedure: Have children draw a picture in pencil and put dots and numbers on it. Now have them erase the lines around their picture. Each child passes his dot picture around the room for others to complete by connecting numbered dots.

Variation: Give children a page filled with randomly numbered dots. Without drawing, they must create a picture by numbering other dots. Children then exchange and complete the connect-the-dot pictures.

DREAM PLACE

Objective: **To help clarify ideals and goals.**

Materials: Paper, pencils, crayons.

Procedure: Have children design to their own satisfaction, a place in which they would like to live. Tell them to make their own rules, regulations, and laws. Tell them to design signs for the place and uses for the signs.

Variation: Have each child think of ten specific things that could be changed in the place that he or she now lives to make it more perfect.

MAKE A BATTLEFIELD

Objective: **To better envision past events.**

Materials: Cardboard, sticks, other materials to make facsimiles.

Procedure: Children and teacher work together to turn a section of the school yard into the site of a well-known historical battle. Children can read full accounts of the battle to determine what artifacts would remain after the battle. They can determine the dispersion of troops and arms. Weapons can be made from cardboard, sticks and other materials. Dolls or toy soldiers can be dressed in the costumes of the day.

Variation: Have children draw a map of the battlefield based on a narrative read to them or by them.

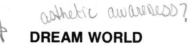

DREAM WORLD

Objective: To introduce and reinforce confidence in personal power to actualize dreams and ambitions.

Materials: Paper, crayons, stories about dreams.

Procedure: Have children close their eyes and think of a dream they have had recently. Ask them to draw the dream or a scene from it. If some have difficulty recalling dreams, pique their memories by reading some familiar stories about dreams, or discussing dreams in popular television programs, movies and plays. Their pictures can be displayed in a dreamland collage or on the bulletin board.

Variation: Have children draw a scene from a dream or a daydream they would like to have.

MOOD MUSIC

Objective: To develop ability to interpret mood as perceived in one mode of expression and to translate it into another expressive mode.

Materials: Paper, pencils, an assortment of records.

Procedure: Play selections from various recordings (suggesting different moods). Have the older children write and the younger children act out their interpretations of the moods conveyed by the music. Then, after playing one selection through several times, ask the children to draw what they hear and feel.

Variation: While children draw a mural based on their study of a particular culture, play recordings representative of that culture's musical heritage.

A SENSE OF COMPLETION

Objective: To increase perception of missing or incomplete elements.

Materials: Colored chalk, blackboard.

Procedure: While children are out of the room, draw several pictures of objects with missing parts on the board. Recall the children and let them take turns creating pictures by drawing in the missing elements. Discuss the varying possibilities. (Note: This requires little real artistic ability on the teacher's part for simple shapes and stick figures serve the purpose. However, for a more sophisticated drawing, coloring book figures can be reproduced with an opaque projector. White liquid paper, familiar to typists, or white poster paint can be used to eliminate parts of the drawings.) Follow up with observation walks in which children list missing things in the real world (e.g., burned out light bulbs, cars without parts).

Variation: While the children are out of the room remove a number of readily noticeable objects or parts of objects. Have children sketch the missing objects.

WEATHER CALENDARS

Objective: To increase originality in creating symbols to represent ideas.

Materials: Paper, crayons.

Procedure: Have each child make a calendar for a month. Then each day have him or her record the weather using his or her own symbols and pictures. Disallow the standard symbols used on television and in the newspapers and instead encourage inventiveness. Post the finished maps on a bulletin board—if possible where other groups of children will notice. Have the students also make a weather prediction for the following month and keep separate tallies of each child's accuracy.

Variation: Have children make calendars and devise symbols to represent the day's outstanding event.

MUSICAL CODE

Objective: To encourage word play and develop sensitivity to the music of language.

Materials: A piano (or other keyboard instrument or a keyboard chart), tape, cards, felt-tip markers.

Procedure: Have children pick one note on the piano as the starting point and label this note with the letter *A*. Then, moving in either direction they label all sequential notes with the rest of the letters of the alphabet using small cards and tape with the letters written on them. (The black keys may be included or left out.) Each child then writes a short sentence or chooses one from a book. They play the sentences on the piano to see what melodies are produced. For variation, children can play newspaper headlines, famous quotes, add punctuation marks to the keyboard, or try to create musical rhythms consistent with the meanings of the words.

Variations:
1. Label each note with a word from a spelling or vocabulary list. Read sentences containing the words but play the word rather than say it.
2. Use a number code instead of letter codes and have children do arithmetic exercises.
3. Have children send musical code messages.

JELLY BEAN CONSTRUCTION

Objective: **To encourage children to take advantage of serendipitous opportunities in creating.**

Materials: Drawing compasses, or long pins, toothpicks, jelly beans.

Procedure: Give each child a compass, a pile of toothpicks, some jelly beans—and creation can begin. Make a base by putting a jelly bean on each end of a toothpick. (If the jelly bean does not readily go into the toothpick, pierce it first with a compass point.) Continue to add toothpicks and jelly beans until a definite pattern is formed. Let the children name their work and write a story about it.

Variation: Have children make a jelly bean mosaic by glueing jelly bean pictures together on cardboard.

INK PATTERNS

Objective: **To promote creativity through experimentation.**

Materials: Washable ink, colored construction paper, newspaper, drinking straws.

Procedure: Cover the work area with newspaper. Place construction paper on the newspaper and give each child some ink and a straw. Tell them to spill a few drops of ink on the paper and with the straw blow ink into random patterns. When they are finished have them title their creations. In subsequent efforts encourage them to follow the flow of the ink and experiment with various types of papers, poster paints and other coloring liquids.

Variation: On an ink pad have the children make designs using finger and thumb prints.

CLASSIFICATION BOXES

Objective: **To develop classification skills.**

Materials: Several boxes (cigar boxes or snack cans are ideal), paper, assorted buttons, a variety of objects of different shapes, colors and material (e.g., marbles, dice, erasers, nuts and bolts, bottle caps, coins, spools).

Procedure: Ask the children to decorate the boxes by covering them with paper and drawing or glueing a picture on the lid representing the category of objects each contains. Have children sort the objects according to size, shape, color, texture, function, or material substance. Then fill the boxes with the appropriate objects.

Variation: Have children make scrapbooks each containing similarly categorized pictures.

SCRAMBLED LEGS

Objective: To develop children's awareness of the structure of language.

Materials: Construction paper or large cards, pencils, scissors, string or tape.

Procedure: Ask each child to write one letter each on two pieces of paper or large cards. (Assign letters so that there is one of every consonant and several of each vowel.) After attaching a card to each leg have the children form two or three lines. At a given signal they scramble to form two new lines. Then one child in each line is selected to write a sentence (nonsense sentences will do) using only the letters from their own line.

Variation: 1. Have the children compete to write the single longest word.
2. Have the children write an entire word on each card. Then the scrambled lines can be used to make longer sentences.

WHAT COLUMBUS FEARED MOST

Objective: To understand better that the unknown often creates an exaggerated sense of fear.

Materials: Large crayons, 18-by-24-inch Manila paper, colored chalk or tempera paint and brush.

Procedure: Talk about the reasons why Columbus and his crew feared a trip to the New World. Explain that the unknown sea monsters and demons feared by the crew were actually species of fish unfamiliar to them at the time. Ask the students to imagine that they are members of Columbus' crew and let them draw huge, scary sea monsters on Manila paper, coloring them as they like. Display the monsters and help the children give them names and labels. The large paper and the other suggested materials will emphasize the monsters' size and allow the children to make sweeping movements without worrying about detail.

Variation: Draw monsters lurking in other frightening places such as outer space, or caves. Or have the children draw their own impressions of specific monsters such as Big Foot, the Abominable Snowman, or the Loch Ness Monster.

NAME PUZZLE

Objective: **To develop a flexible and experimental attitude toward designs.**

Materials: Cardboard, drawing compass, pencil, tempera paint, brush, scissors.

Procedure: Use a sturdy piece of cardboard and draw the largest possible circle with a compass. When this is done, have the children print their name in the circle from top to bottom using the entire circle. Next have the children color in the spaces of their name with several colors of tempera paint. The name will become a design. When the paint has dried, tell the children to cut the circle into various shapes and sizes. The pieces should not be too small. Each child will put his puzzle in a bag with his name on it.

Variation: Have the children cut the circle into pieces based on the lines and broken spaces. They can then use it as a puzzle.

STAND-ON MUSIC

Objective: **To develop positive and imaginative attitudes toward reading and composing music.**

Materials: Wide roll paper (white banquet table type or brown wrapping paper), colored pencil or felt-tip marking pens.

Procedure: Make a musical staff as wide as the paper by drawing five horizontal lines. Make sure the lines are spaced equally over the entire length of the paper. Have the children pretend to be individual notes by standing either on a line or between the lines. Explain that together they represent the musical score. Play or sing these "people notes" and then have the children change positions.

Variations: 1. Have the children assume the appropriate positions on the staff for a line of music from a familiar song.
2. In a class of older children, one member can be a flat, natural, or sharp and change the sound of the person he or she stands by. Children can also illustrate the relative duration of sounds by pretending to be whole-notes, half-notes, and quarter-notes.

IT'S SNOW GO

Objective: **To develop imaginative inventive abilities.**

Materials: Crayons, 12-inch or 18-inch Manila paper, scissors, paste, construction paper, price tags, soap, blunt knives.

Procedure: Have the children design their own super snow vehicle using crayons and Manila paper. Suggest to the children that the vehicles be adaptable for driving on ice as well as snow. Each should be made for speed and be large enough to seat at least two passengers. When the vehicles are finished, tell the children to cut them out and paste them on colored construction paper. Display the pictures with price tags and have each child pretend to be a salesman. Invite another class to come in and visit the display posing as potential purchasers.

Variations:
1. Suggest that the children carve their vehicles out of soap. Some might prefer to use wood or cardboard.
2. Have the children design the vehicle for a favorite comic book or television heroine or hero.

SMELLING UP THE PLACE

Objective: **To increase ability to use various senses in imaginative ways.**

Materials: Six or seven bags that contain different smelling substances (perfume, soap), paper, pencils, crayons.

Procedure: Discuss the sense of smell. Pass the bags around the room and tell the children to open the bags, smell once, then close them and pass them on. Have children draw a picture of what they smelled. The picture should not simply illustrate what is in the bag, but should depict something about the object, where it came from, what it is used for, or what it reminds them of. The bags must be kept closed except when in use and should be scattered in the room so the smells will not get mixed. After the children draw their pictures, the bags are sniffed again and the smells identified.

Variation: Read several "scratch-and-sniff" type books. Have children write and illustrate their own "scratch-and-sniff" story to be read to a preschool child. Use sniff bags or lidded sniff cans instead of scratch spots.

FRACTIONAL PARTS

Objective: **To develop a better sense of fractional relationships.**

Materials: White pieces of paper cut into circles, crayons.

Procedure: Give each student a circular piece of paper. Have the students fold these in half and color the two exposed sides a light shade of red. Then ask each student to fold the paper in half again and shade the two exposed parts a darker red. The shape should be folded again and the small pieces shaded even darker. Have the students study the results and determine as many fractional relationships as they can. Make a list of these relationships.

Example:

two-halves
four-fourths   } in a whole
eight-eighths

two-fourths   } in a half
four-eighths

six-eighths   } three-fourths

Variation: Experiment with ovals, squares, stars, and irregular shapes.

CHRISTMAS TREES

Objective: **To increase appreciation for the creative beauty of ornamented Christmas trees.**

Materials: Green paint, 18-by-24-inch Manila paper, assorted construction paper, scissors, paste.

Procedure: Tell the children to paint the largest possible Christmas tree on the 18-by-24-inch paper. While the paint dries have them cut paper ornaments and a base that can be added to the Christmas tree. Have them paste the ornaments on the tree and cut it out.

Variations:
1. Use ornaments as symbols to tell a Christmas story.
2. Decorate the tree in the tradition of some other culture.
3. Paint and ornament trees other than evergreens.

🦃 HOLIDAY SWITCH

Objective: **To develop ability to imagine things differently than they really are.**

Procedure: Have the children switch the symbols associated with one holiday to another holiday and try to imagine how the symbols would be changed. For example: What would an Easter or Valentine tree look like? What about Halloween eggs? What would you get "trick or treating" on St. Patrick's Day? They can paint or draw their own versions of these switched symbols or create three dimensional structures and sculptures using egg cartons, plastic straws, and other materials.

Variation: Have children create an entirely new symbol for a holiday.

HALLOWEEN FRIENDS

Objective: **To create artistically imaginative expressions of holidays.**

Materials: Newspaper, orange and black paint, scissors, paste, gray or black paper.

Procedure: Talk with the children about the different things associated with Halloween such as witches, bats, owls, ghosts, goblins, pumpkins, and black cats. Have the children paint pictures using only orange and black paint on newspaper. When the pictures are finished mount them on black or gray paper.

Variation: Have the children design Halloween want ads or wanted posters.

STONES

Objective: **To increase ability to visualize an object as something else or in another function.**

Materials: Felt-tip markers, felt, paste.

Procedure: Have the children bring interestingly shaped stones to school. Let each child choose one stone. Suggest that they examine it from all angles and try to imagine the stone becoming something—a rabbit, cat, dog, etc. Have them use felt-tip markers to accentuate the animal shapes. Tell them to draw portions of the body if the stone's shape lends itself readily to ink drawing. Stop here unless some of the children want to cut and paste pieces of felt on the stone to represent the animal's ears or other features.

Variations:
1. Have the children imagine the stone as a kind of stained glass window. Using black paint or felt-tip marker draw lines to separate and section the stone. Then color in the sections.
2. Have the children pretend the stone is a secret identifying symbol carried by messengers of a government agency. What would the decorations on the stone show?
3. Have the children pretend the stone has magical qualities and decorate it accordingly.

PAPER BEADS

Objective: **To develop ability to create from a set patterned activity.**

Materials: Lightweight paper, glue, thin round sticks.

Procedure: Have the children cut the paper into long thin triangular shapes. The widest end will be the length of the bead. Beginning with this end roll the paper triangle tightly around a thin stick. After the pointed end is glued fast, remove the stick. When the glue has dried paint the bead a solid color or decorate it with an interesting design. The beads can be strung or used to make a stained glass or mosaic type sculpture.

Variation: Experiment with paper triangles of different lengths and widths. Also wind them around objects of varying shapes and sizes.

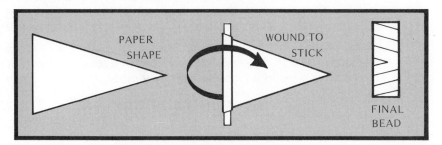

PAINTING ABSTRACTS

Objective: **To develop an experimental attitude toward art.**

Materials: Paper towels, white paste, 9-by-12-inch cardboard, water, paint, brushes.

Procedure: Demonstrate the activity for the children before they begin. Use warm colors for the winter, cool for spring and summer. Cover a sheet of cardboard with a layer of paste. Wet a paper towel, squeeze it damp dry, and start to attach it to the pasted cardboard. Do not lay it flat, but push it up into the paste. When one towel is attached, add another until the cardboard is completely covered with crinkled towels. Let the towels dry and then paint them. Mingle the colors in some areas to produce exciting effects.

Variations:
1. After thinning the paint, experiment with different application methods (sprayer or spray bottle, medicine dropper, sponge, potato sliced in half with a design carved on the flat surface).
2. Mix the paint with varying substances (soap flakes, sand, melted wax) to see how its changed consistency and texture affects application.

 SPAGHETTI ART

Objective: **To develop the ability to use unusual materials creatively.**

Materials: Cooked spaghetti, food coloring, construction paper.

Procedure: Place the spaghetti in separate bowls and put food coloring in each. Use four colors of food coloring. Then give each child a large piece of construction paper. The children can create pictures, designs, or write words using the spaghetti. Tell the children to pick it up carefully one strand at a time. If the spaghetti is dropped, it will not stick to the paper. Allow each paper to dry thoroughly.

Variation: Create mosaics using different sizes and shapes of macaroni.

DOUGH BOYS

Objective: To provide opportunity for self-expression.

Materials: Each child should have one cup flour, ½ cup salt, ½ cup or more water, waxed paper, paint, brushes.

Procedure: Have children mix the dough to a pliable but firm consistency. Then place the dough on a piece of waxed paper and create various shapes (abstract, geometrical, solid). For variety the children can make faces using additional pieces of dough to represent the nose, chin, eyebrows, eyes, and mouth. Ask the children to make a hole in their projects so that they can be hung later on. When the ornaments are finished, they should be set aside about a week to dry; or they can be baked in the oven at four-hundred degrees until they are brown. If they are baked, broken bits of hard candy like sour balls or lollipops can be added to open areas of the dough. These become transparent colored areas when the baked pieces are cold. The ornaments can also be painted.

Variation: Have children experiment with imprinting using varying tools, coins, etc. on flattened surfaces of the dough.

MAP INVENTING

Objective: To develop a keener awareness of the features found on maps and in specific geographic areas.

Procedure: Ask the students to name as many different maps as possible. List these on the blackboard. Choose one kind of map from the list to talk about, for example, a state map. Ask the students to name things they would expect to find on a state map and list these on the board. Draw a shape on the chalkboard to represent an imaginary state. Have the students start planning the state by referring to the list describing what information a state map should convey. The teacher should guide the discussion by asking questions like: "Where will be a good place for the mountains? Why? What should be near the mountains? Why? How many people live in the state? What do the people do for a living? What kind of land areas are in the state? Where can people go for a vacation within the state? What is the main industry? Why? What are the natural resources?"

Variation: Have children "replan" an existing state or other area placing man-made and natural sites in *better* locations than they think they are in currently.

MR. NORTH WIND

Objective: To develop ability to express nonvisual perceptions in visual forms.

Materials: Blue crayon, white paint, brushes, newspaper, and 12-by-18-inch dark-blue paper.

Procedure: Tell the students to draw their interpretations of the north wind on blue paper with the blue crayon. (Press hard with the crayon.) In some of the pictures fill in whole areas of blue so the picture is more than an outline drawing. Dilute white paint with water using the ratio two parts paint to three parts water. Put newspaper under the picture. Paint over the entire picture with the diluted white paint. The paint will adhere to the paper but not to the crayoned areas. Bend the paper into a cylindrical shape, stapling the ends. Attach a strip of blue paper to make a handle and hang the cylinders from the ceiling in clusters.

Variation: Have the children use this resist technique to represent their interpretations of other weather conditions (tornado, monsoon, thunderstorm, drought).

SEEING THE UNSEEN

Objective: **To develop observation skills and the ability to reproduce and represent observed detail.**

Materials: Paper, crayons.

Procedure: Talk with the class about things they see everyday on the way to school and in the classroom. Ask if there is something they have seen lately that was really beautiful and if they tried to get someone else to see it. Tell them that sometimes people look at things without *really* seeing them. For this day, ask them to purposely try to notice something that is beautiful, or something they think nobody else sees. Have the children look out of the window and describe what they see. After this take them outside for a short time and encourage them to really look at the things they see. After coming back inside, give everyone paper and crayons to draw pictures. Discourage conversation. When the pictures are finished, go back outside to discuss them. Ask the children if they can find what their classmates saw. On another day the search might be for especially small things, for parts of things that are not hidden, or for things that are not usually noticed.

Variation: Have a child draw some particular detail of a complex object or series of objects that all other class members are looking directly at. See who can identify it.

LISTEN AND SEE

Objective: **To increase awareness of sensory interrelationships.**

Materials: A bell, colored construction paper, paste, white paper, scissors, colored chalk.

Procedure: Ask the children if they have ever seen a sound. Tell them they have seen lots of sounds. While the class closes its eyes, ring a bell. When they open their eyes ask them what they heard. Ask how they knew it was a bell—because it sounded like one. Discuss the mental image of a bell produced by the sound. Explain that this was "seeing a sound". Ask the children what sounds they have "seen" on their way to school—trains, cars, airplanes, birds. Ask them, "Do sounds have color?" "Would the sound of a cat purring have the same color as a dog barking?" Discuss sounds that are soft; these would be represented by soft colors and heavy sounds by dark colors.

Things we see are made up of lines and shapes as well as color. Have someone draw a "sound wave" line on the blackboard to represent a dog barking—then a cat purring. Talk about the differences. Discuss other sounds and what they look like. Compare them. Give each child a piece of colored construction paper. Ask them to cut out an image of the thing that makes the sound. Paste this on a large piece of white paper and with colored chalk draw what the sound looks like within the thing.

Variation: Have children experiment drawing smells, tastes, or the way things feel when touched.

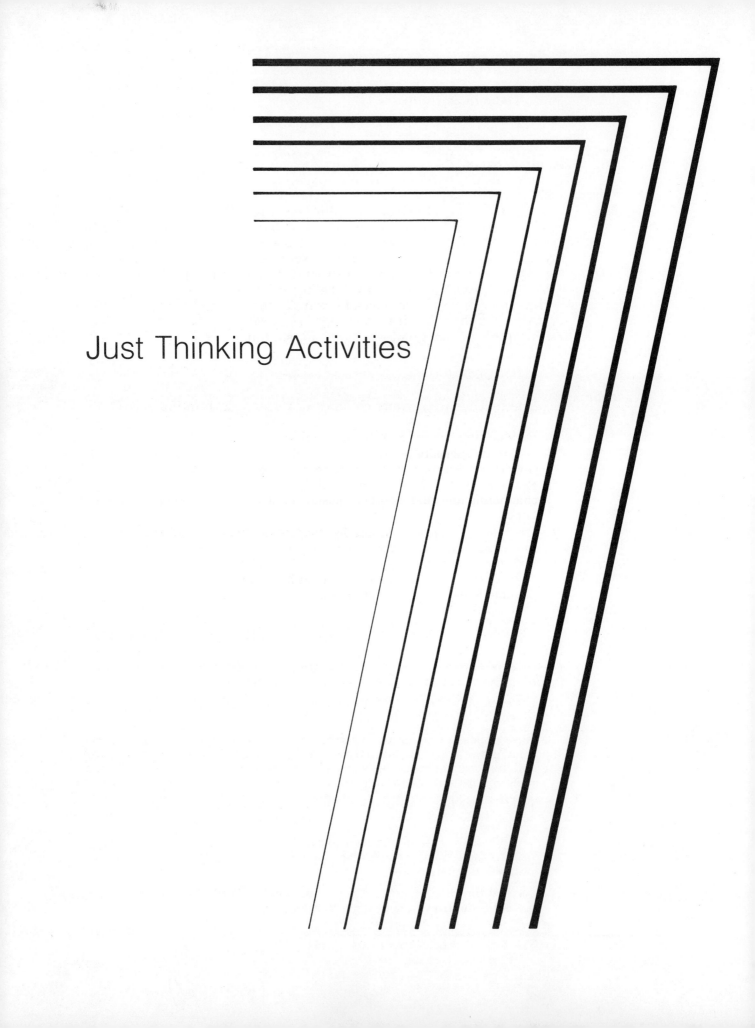

Just Thinking Activities

Many writers describe creativity as a problem-solving process, one of thinking about and trying to find new and different solutions to problems. Thought is the basis of all creativity. The writer, inventor, artist, or musician must make countless decisions and overcome innumerable problems in the course of his or her work. There is a creative joy, a sense of accomplishment in overcoming past frustration, in finding escape from impasse, and reaching that moment of discovery. Fantasy, logic, curiosity, imagination, and invention are the principal thinking tools through which that joy is found.

A child can have the pleasure of creating without producing some product for an audience to see and even without any visible action. This kind of creation originates in the palaces of the mind. Teachers cannot grade it nor can schools measure it. Nonetheless, education cannot afford to fail in providing opportunities for the child to do just this kind of thinking. Rather than hastily labeling it as day-dreaming, teachers, parents and schools should look for ways of encouraging and channeling fantasy thought into directions that help growth and aid the child in reaching his or her greatest potential as a human being.

ANTI-ROBOT PATROL

The teacher who wants children to turn on to thinking should:

1. Provide time for children to just think.
2. Stimulate curiosity by surrounding children with unanswered questions, problems to solve, and unexplained mysteries.
3. Respond to questions in an encouraging manner by answering some, channeling and guiding others, posing for others, and denying response to none.
4. Encourage impossible dreams by listening to them sympathetically.
5. Encourage the formulation of multiple hypotheses and alternative solutions to problems.
6. Do not try to be the expert or the authority on all things. As much as possible leave that to the children.

CREATIVE THINGS FOR CHILDREN TO DO WITH A BLANK ISLAND MAP

1. Have children put in their own geographic features such as rivers, mountains, marshes, deserts, forests, meadows, volcanoes, cliffs.

2. Let each child locate all the natural and man-made features that would make the island a perfect place for them to live.

3. Have children pretend to be a group of pioneer colonists (at any point in time) going to the island to live. They must assess the island's geographical features to determine where they will settle. Ask them to defend the reasons for their choices.

4. Tell the children that a pirate captain has buried his/her treasure on the island. Have them draw the treasure map.

5. Give children a menu of a pioneer family's meals during one week. Have the children then draw in the features the island must have and the vegetation it must support.

6. Pretend that the island is a "fairy tale land" or "tall tale land" and have the children draw in the sights they would see.

7. Have children plan a theme-based amusement park for the island (such as Frontier World, Gay 90's, Sea Land).

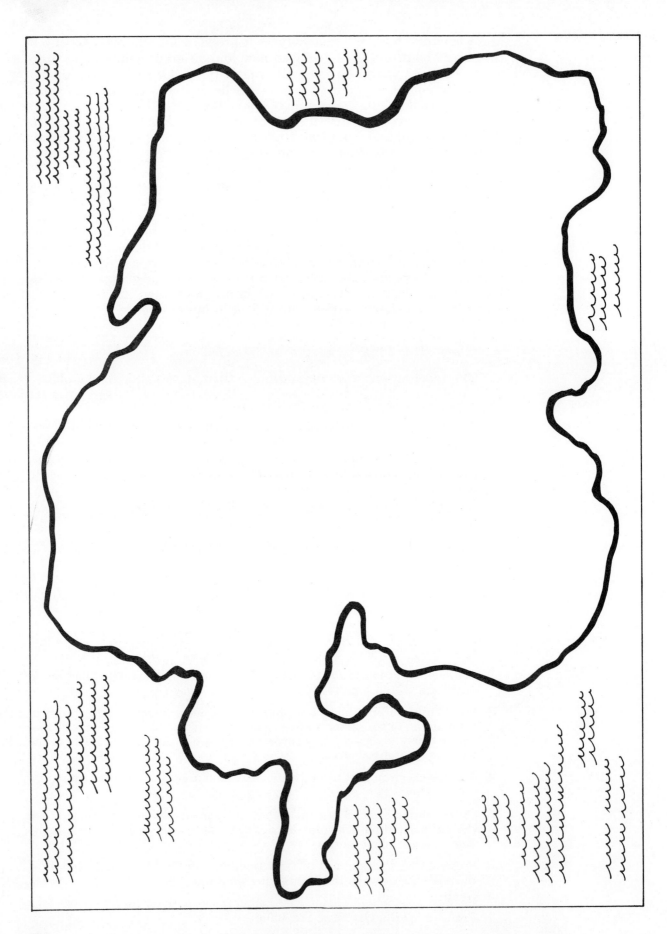

124

8. After a discussion on energy problems, have the children make the island into the model site for future energy conservation practices.

9. Tell the children that the island is being set up as a trial community to better human relationships. Let them dream up their own alternative approaches to accomplish this goal. Here are two ideas they might like to consider: (1) each major country has a piece of land; (2) each major nation sends two people to live on the island. How would these settlers form a friendly and mutually beneficial community?

10. Organize the island as a model prison. Who would go there? How would it be different from current penal facilities?

11. Assign each child, pair of children or small group a culture or civilization. They are to pretend that their civilization is founding a colony on the island and that they can build only ten structures. What structures would they build? In what order would they build them?

12. Think of a particular culture group and climate for the island. Have children ask questions about the island and its people which can be answered yes or no. As they receive yes answers have them draw symbols on the island map representing what they have learned. At the end of a set period (five minutes) or number of questions, have the children summarize their composite picture of the island.

CREATIVE THINGS FOR CHILDREN TO DO WITH A BLANK ROAD MAP OF A DENSELY POPULATED AREA

1. Have children determine what community helpers are needed and where they will be located.

2. Give children directional instructions concerning sites to locate on the maps. (e.g., there is a school in the northeast quarter of the town.)

3. Have children pretend that their maps show a subdivision with streets being named to correspond to a particular theme. (They can choose their own.) For example, all the streets might be named for presidents, states, or trees.

4. Treat the map as though it were the area of a town where a story they have read took place. Have them label the locations important to the story.

5. Tell the children to pretend they are going to buy a home somewhere in this section of town. They are to think of the things they want to be near (such as schools or particular stores), and the things they want to be sure they are far away from (such as busy streets, etc.). It is important *not* to condition the children with examples. (Some examples also might make the children ashamed of their own home location.)

6. Have children make the town into the ideal place to shop by locating on the map all the stores they might need. Thought should be given to the relative size of stores and to the number of stores of the *same* kind.

7. Let children pretend that this is a community of the future and show how it would be different.

8. Many stories describe animals that seem nearly human. Have the children pretend that this town represents a particular animal community (e.g., ants, rabbits, birds). The maps should indicate the special needs of this community.

9. Assign to each group of children a type of community (military, industrial, wealthy, or poor); ethnically, religiously, or culturally unified. Have them show how the community map might reflect these groupings.

10. Have children pretend that this is a special purpose community. The purpose may be realistic (e.g., garment production, or tourist attraction), or unrealistic and fantastic (producing the ingredients for magic potions, brews and charms).

GIANTS

Objective: **To develop empathy for small living things.**

Procedure: Ask children to think about how small creatures living in the grass feel about the giantlike humans who walk all over their world. What does a flower represent to these creatures? Let children try to imagine themselves as an insect or a small animal looking up at humans. Discuss feelings and actions. As a follow-up activity pantomime to jungle music.

Variation: Have children think about how giant creatures such as whales and elephants and powerful creatures such as lions, tigers, and poisonous snakes would feel toward a child. They can imagine themselves as each of these animals in turn.

ANTIBIOTIC

Objective: **To help growth in understanding of the human body.**

Procedure: Have children imagine that they are an antibiotic that has just been injected into a human body. What would they experience and what battles would they fight?

Variation: Children can imagine that they are corpuscles or certain parts of the body encountering various problems or germs. This can be turned into an action story in which each child adds a sentence or two that requires some action. The whole class participates in the action.

ANIMAL COMBINATIONS

Objective: **To develop ability to imagine strange combinations.**

Procedure: Have children imagine how combination animals would look:

elepheagle	hippoduckamus
kangarooster	canarigoat
octopussycat	tigerilla

As a follow-up activity, have them draw these strange animals or write descriptions of them.

Variation: Try the combining game with a homemade deck of cards, each picturing a different plant or animal. When they get two animals or two plants they describe the combination and coin a name.

BECOMING PRESIDENT

Objective: **To help build understanding that power has responsibility.**

Procedure: As a thought provoker, ask the question: "If you ran for president and you actually won the election, what would be your first goal? How would you go about it?" Children might further brainstorm lists of things they would change; wouldn't change; couldn't change.

Variations:
1. Have children imagine themselves head of state of any place in the world at any time in history. Ask them to explain their choice and describe what they could do.
2. Have children imagine they are members of the president's cabinet. What position would they hold? What advice would they give the president? What program would they want to develop?

IS IN WHAT?

Objective: To increase visualization of relative space and understanding of spatial concepts.

Procedure: Have children close their eyes and tell them to think of a simple symbol for each of the following steps. "The state is in the nation; the nation is in the world; the world is in the solar system; the solar system is in the universe; the universe is in what?" Let them try to make a mental image of each step. For some children it might be well to start with even smaller units. For example: "They are in the room; the room is in the school; the school is in the block; the block is in the community; the community is in the town; the town is in the county, etc." Simple geometric shapes of different colors are one way of helping the visualization process.

Variations:
1. Use time: "A second is in a minute; a minute is in an hour; an hour is in a day; a day is in a week; a week is in a month; a month is in a year; a year is in a decade."
2. Use matter: "An atom is in a molecule; a molecule is in a grain (or drop, etc)." This can be varied by changing the object (a tree, the earth, etc.).
3. Reverse the process and go from larger to smaller units.
4. Use this activity as a "larger-than" game or a card game.

THE NEW KING'S NUMBER NOTES

Objective: To develop ability to rename concepts and symbols.

Procedure: Children should pretend that a new king has come to this country. He becomes furious at number words that we have now. He has promised half the kingdom and a month-long trip to Hawaii and Disneyland to anyone who will invent a logical new set of names for the numbers: 1, 2, 3, 4, 5, 6, 7, 8, 9, 10, 11, 12, etc.; as well as the mathematical signs: $+ \div \times - \sqrt{}$, and measures (either metric or nonmetric).

Variation: Let the children create new signs and symbols for numbers. Then let them try to compute using their system.

MAGIC AUCTION

Objective: To clarify personal values about relative worth.

Materials: Play money, auction lists and price lists or catalogues.

Procedure: Divide children in groups of three to five. Give each group "markers" for the same amount of money (say $10,000). Play auction games in which they bid their sums on agreed on choices. They need to see the complete list of items beforehand and have time to talk about them and decide on strategy. (Children might like to make up their own currency beforehand.) Give the children "tickets" representing their winning bids. Afterwards discuss their choices and the reasoning behind these as well as strategies.

Variations:
1. Have children keep track of their spendings in a record form without markers of any type.
2. Have children brainstorm their own lists of auctionable items.
3. Use a catalogue or price list and pick things with real value. Let groups try to get the best bargain for their money.

ONCE UPON A MILLIONAIRE

Objective: **To develop a sense of relative worth.**

Procedure: Each student pretends he is given a million dollars. He must find something to spend it on. However, he must invest in something that will not make a profit. This leaves out stocks, bonds, business enterprises, and other such ventures. This task is designed to stretch the students' thinking ability about money and personal economic values. They must somehow establish the current prices of the items on their investment list.

Variation: Have students hypothetically spend a specific amount on items selected from a given catalogue. Permit them *no* cost overrun and only a certain amount under cost. They must figure tax and shipping.

THE LONG WEEKEND HOLIDAY

Objective: **To clarify reasons for holidays and their importance.**

Procedure: Ask students to make up an imaginary holiday and have them answer such questions as:
When will the holiday be and what will it be called?
Who will celebrate the holiday?
What forms will the celebration take?
What will symbolize this holiday?
How will people commemorate the day? (cards, gifts, etc.)

Variation: Have students imagine what holidays would be celebrated by various groups of animals or by mythical creatures (such as elves or ghosts). They might begin by imagining holidays corresponding to ours. (What would be their Independence Day? Columbus Day? etc.)

TAKING MEASUREMENTS

Objective: **To develop a sense of relative size.**

Procedure: Give the students the task of measuring the school playground or parts of the building. Ask them to find different ways of accurately recording these dimensions without relying on standard units or measuring instruments (rulers, meter sticks, measuring tapes). They might, for example, originate measuring units based on something they have at hand (desks, notebook paper, etc.) Encourage estimating and comparison.

Variation: Have students measure smaller things using the fractional parts of larger things as measuring units. (e.g., the classroom is 1/10 as long as the school or it takes 12 jelly beans to equal the width of an index card.)

UNDERWATER HOUSE

Objective: **To develop adaptive thinking and vision.**

Procedure: Have students think of a design for an underwater house. Ask them what they will see if they look out the windows. What happens when they open the door? How will they breathe, be transported to the surface, or get food?

Variation: Allow students to brainstorm about houses in other impossible locations (in space, in the center of the sun, or in the center of solid rock).

KALEIDOSCOPE

Objective: To increase descriptive power and the ability to translate visual perceptions into verbal expressions.

Materials: A kaleidoscope.

Procedure: Allow students to look in a kaleidoscope for a few minutes. For each picture have them think of a different word to describe it. For each design have them make up a nonsense word that might describe it.

Variations: Write a story, make up a song, or paint a picture about a kaleidoscope's personality or changeability.

COLOR IMAGES

storytelling

Objective: To develop ability to envision colors representing moods.

Materials: *Hailstones and Halibut Bones* by Mary O'Neil or other books of poetry.

Procedure: Read O'Neil's *Hailstones and Halibut Bones* to help extend students' color concepts. Next, ask the class to imagine colors representing words with emotional meanings such as:

angry	soft	hot
happy	rough	cool
sad	hard	huge

Variation: Have children imagine colors and/or shapes and/or numbers which could represent times like holidays, days of the week, or seasons; or idea words like love, reverence, beauty. They might write short poems in haiku or couplet form.

ENEMIES MEET

Objective: **To stimulate sensory imagery related to nonsensory ideas and feelings, and to enlarge the dimensions of personal reality.**

Materials: Illustrated books of myths and legends.

Procedure: Stimulate children to imagine what various emotions individual people have. Have them describe what love, hate, fear, indifference, etc. would look like; what their facial expression would be, what activities they would take part in. Then have children think of situations and instances when two emotions meet (e.g., similar ones like indifference and apathy or opposites like enthusiasm and boredom). Why could both examples of similar (or opposite) emotions be enemies at such a meeting? Afterwards read some of the myths which tell of gods which represent qualities.

Variation: Have students draw, make a straw or clay model, or enact the confrontations.

PUTTING YOURSELF INTO THINGS

Objective: **To develop ability to envision viewpoints other than one's own.**

Procedure: Have students close their eyes and think about a particular object. Now, have them imagine that they *are* this thing. After they open their eyes, they may tell what they thought about, describe how the thing looked at the world around, the limitations of being the thing, its wishes, angers, frustrations.

Variation: Have students each describe the "thing's" views, attitudes, or feelings without naming it. Let the other children guess.

PICTORIAL RIDDLES

Objective: **To increase the question-asking abilities and curiosity of children.**

Materials: Paper, pencil, paints, crayons, and glue.

Procedure: A pictorial riddle is a riddle presented in picture form. Riddles can illustrate an actual situation or a situation which has been altered so that one can state what is wrong. Have students make up their own riddles. Some picture riddles simply illustrate the idea involved in a verbal question. For example, why are two rubber plungers difficult to pull apart when the cups are pushed tightly together? Other examples: Why do Ping Pong balls bounce but not marbles? Why does water go around in a circle before going down the drain? In some cases, the pictures are sufficient in themselves because they create a sense of incompleteness. Picture puzzles may also be used in code messages, rebuses, and picture perception exercises. The most common types of picture perception exercises are those which ask children to spot the mistakes in a picture or to pick out pictures hidden within a picture.

Variations: Have children speculate about pictures, especially different kinds of photos. Ask such questions as:
1. What location do the pictures show?
2. What idea(s) do they represent?
3. If the pictures were made a few minutes (hours, weeks) later or earlier what differences would there have been?

THE MASTER DETECTIVE

Objective: To arouse curiosity and stimulate speculation about alternative solutions to a problem.

Procedure: Children have watched countless mysteries on television. Give them a chance to "backtrack" the detective. In the statements below the detective tells what led him/her to solve each crime. Discuss with the children various possibilities to which these statements could refer.

"It was not what was in the room that told me who committed the crime but what was *not* in the room."

"There was never any doubt who did it. The only question was how they did it."

"What the victim wore on the day of the crime was the important clue in the case."

"He didn't mean to tell me that he committed the crime, but that is just exactly what he did."

"The victim actually told everyone who committed the crime. They just failed to understand him."

Variation: Build classroom mysteries about a particular person or thing in the room. The clues might refer to things that happened the previous day. Additional clues can be added each day.

NEW FABLES

Objective: **To increase power to argue and convince by example and illustration.**

Materials: Books containing various types of fables and moral tales. Lists of "wise" sayings.

Procedure: Read a selected fable to the class. A fable is a short narrative which teaches a lesson or makes a single moral point. Often fables have animal characters but the animals talk and are much like human beings. Have the children work "backwards" beginning with the "lesson" and then generating an incident in which characters "prove" the lesson by their example. Well-known proverbs and maxims make good starters for fables. The whole class or small groups can work together on the new fable, beginning from a common point in the discussion.

Variations:
1. Have children evolve parables and moral rules.
2. Have children "prove" with a fable exemplar something they believe is not true.

MAGIC MATH MACHINE

Objective: **To apply concepts and processes learned in math.**

Procedure: Draw and demonstrate your own pretend machine. This machine does mysterious things to numbers. Drop a seven into it and out will come fifteen. Drop a three into it and out will come seven. Drop a two into it and out will come five. What will come out if you put five into the machine? Answer: The machine doubles the number and adds one to it. Have the students design machines and make up their own processes. Try using division, subtraction, or multiplication.

Variation: Build a front for the machine out of a refrigerator box or other large cardboard box. A child sits behind the box. Other children feed the machine numbers by calling them out. The child in the box feeds out the "processed" math through a slot cut in the front. When a child guesses how the machine works he/she gets to go inside.

STREAM OF THOUGHT

Objective: To develop better understanding of thinking processes.

Materials: Pencil and paper.

Procedure: Have students write down a single word every five to ten seconds. This word can be randomly chosen or one that sums up what they have been thinking. Continue for at least ten minutes. Now have students trace their thought pattern. Talk about questions such as: What outside influences changed your train of thought? What inward influences did you notice having an effect?

Variation: Have children write as rapidly as they can in a stream of consciousness style without giving thought to spelling, punctuation, sentence structure, or cohesion, for a limited period of time.

HAPPY CENTURY

Objective: To help in developing understanding for others.

Procedure: Tell students to pretend that they are celebrating their 100th birthday. Let them speculate about the things they would be thinking. This can lead to a writing or role-playing activity.

Variation: Have children talk about the memories a hundred-year-old person might have and think up questions that might help bring these memories into focus.

GIVE AND TAKE VALUE

Objective: To develop greater awareness of personal thought processes and value system.

Materials: A collection of ordinary objects such as sticks, chalk, pens, paper clips, crayons, paper bags.

Procedure: Give a student three different objects (for example, a crayon, a bag, and a paper clip). Tell the child to give back any one object and keep two. Ask the child to think about how he/she decided which object to return.

Variations:
1. Have a child choose two objects to give to someone else from among five objects.
2. Have a child select one object to throw away.
3. Have a child with three objects choose one to hold up in the air.

INVENTION ATTENTION

Objective: To increase thought flexibility and originality.

Procedure: Ask each student to create a new product to sell. Each producer must state what currently used item the product will replace as well as the new product's qualities.

Variation: Brainstorm with children in small groups a list of inventions that are needed in today's world, or a list of books that need to be written, or a list of possible new brand names for new products in a given line (car models, cereals, etc).

CLOUD STARE *asthetic*

Objective: To develop power to envision.

Procedure: Have the class go out of doors and stare at a cloud. Ask them to imagine something from the cloud formations. When a pattern is perceived ask the student to be sure to remember it. Afterwards, ask each student to describe the cloud, its formations, and his/her reaction to it.

Variation: Make a series of ink or poster paint blots on paper or use a straw and a thin solution of paint or ink to make a design. Have children see what images they can discern in the designs.

SEEING IT FRAMED

Objective: To increase sensory awareness of aesthetically and intellectually interesting items in the environment.

Procedure: Have the children make mental picture frames around things that catch their eye and imagine these "paintings" upon particular walls of particular buildings. "Frames" formed by making a square with the thumb and forefinger of both hands can help the imagination here. He/she then invites someone else to see the "picture."

Variation: Have children tell about things they remember seeing that they would really like to have kept a picture of.

EMOTIONAL VISION

Objective: To develop ability to project concrete manifestations of emotion.

Procedure: Have students draw a picture of "lovely" or "loveliness" (variations include: peace, love, happiness, joy, trust, loneliness, despair). Begin by imagining the picture and then describing it. The picture may be symbolic or representative and may assume the appearance of a collage.

Variation: Have students each take a mirror and try to show emotion in their facial expressions. Then have them draw representations of these facial expressions.

THE SOUND AND FEEL OF TRAVEL

Objective: To intensify sensory perceptions and awareness of their meanings.

Procedure: While riding as a passenger in a car, bus, airplane, or other vehicle have children close their eyes and concentrate on perceptions of movement. Ask them what sensory impressions inform them about changes in speed and direction and about the vehicle itself. Ask them what the sounds from outside tell them. The moods can be simulated in the classroom using a series of recorded sounds but obviously the movement feelings are lost.

Variation: Have children record a series of sounds and then talk about other sensory impressions they would expect to accompany the sounds.

THE RAFFLE WINNERS

Objective: To develop problem-solving skill.

Procedure: Give children a chance to solve the following problems.
Suppose 1,000 people bought raffle tickets numbered 1–1000 on one first prize, two second prizes, and three third prizes. How could the six winning numbers be chosen in a fair and random way. One approach is to write the numbers 1–1000 on bits of paper, fold them, and put them in a hat. After shaking the hat well, draw out six numbers. But there should be a quicker and better way to choose six numbers at random. Have the children devise a method of doing this. Then try their way ten times and see if the ten choices of six numbers seem to be random. Do any numbers appear more than once? Is there a tendency toward one-digit numbers, or two-digit numbers, or three-digit numbers?

Variation: Have children devise ways of choosing that are *not* random but are based on criteria.

Five Minutes
to Go

At the end of a day, at the end of a period, just before lunch, waiting for call to go to an assembly, waiting for a speaker or another class to come, and at countless other times—there is a little period of waiting. It is a short period, perhaps fifteen minutes long but usually a lot less. It seems there is not enough time to *really* do anything, to start something new, to get out materials. Before anything could really be started it would be time to stop.

But time is precious—children's, teacher's, everyone's. Creativity can claim that few minutes and make it a *useful* learning and growing time. With five minutes to go—a thinking problem can be attacked, a discussion can be conducted, a small group buzz session held. Children can be "conditioned" to expect these quick creating times, even anticipate and look forward to them.

Creativity can still claim that five minutes despite the argument of some teachers that a "quiet" time is needed to keep from having to call the riot squad or worse. Children do need "do nothing" time for relaxing from the pressures of school. They also need a time to get their emotions settled, to readjust, to ready their minds for a coming change. But the safety valve and calmative can be idea productive, fun, and activity involving. This chapter offers a few "quickie" ideas for those many "five minutes to go" times.

To avoid filling those last few minutes with mere busy work, teachers should follow a few simple guidelines. The following rules are simply to remind teachers that children's time is valuable and important, and that five minutes can make or destroy a creative learning environment.

1. Avoid obvious fillers that are contrived and created on the spot. Think ahead! Have ideas prepared and ready. Make the time-takers important.

2. Utilize activities that do not call for confusing class movements or materials to be distributed before starting. The time will disappear before you have really begun.

3. Strive to make short-time activities motivating so that children will look forward to them. Children should see this time as a reward for work well done, not a punishment.

4. Timing is important. Keep the pace natural, neither rushing nor "dragging" the activity.

5. Have types of activities for a few children as well as some for the entire class. The former should be "low distraction" type activities.

The remainder of this chapter describes specific candidate activities to make that little period of waiting rewarding.

THINGS TO DO WITH "THING LISTS"

Several "thing lists" follow. Here are some five-minute things to do with the lists.

1. Do association series.
2. Do association rounds with no repeats allowed.
3. Brainstorm additions to lists of things.
4. Change things on lists putting in better ones or synonyms.
5. Ask a question about each thing.
6. Give an opposite of each thing.

7. Describe each thing.
8. Put the name of each thing on a card. The children choose several cards and combine the words into one story.
9. Pantomime things as a guessing game.
10. Say each thing on the list several times with different facial and vocal expressions.
11. List as many functions as possible of each thing.
12. Tell as many ways as possible that things can be improved by being modified.

THINGS

The physical presence of the objects can be useful in stimulating thought.

1. A box of crackers
2. An old sock
3. An empty tin can
4. A tablet of paper
5. A large cooking pot
6. A ball
7. A sandwich
8. A hammer
9. A toy teddy bear
10. A ball of string

Second-Level Words

11. A block of wood
12. A brick
13. A bell
14. A small jar of paint
15. A water glass
16. A pie pan
17. A needle
18. A ball point pen
19. A flower pot
20. An empty ice cream container

BIG THINGS

1. A car
2. A storm cloud
3. A house
4. A tree
5. A jet plane
6. A school
7. A supermarket
8. An ocean liner
9. A skyscraper
10. An elephant

Second-Level Words

11. A library
12. A mountain
13. A river
14. A desert
15. An ocean
16. An oil well
17. A factory
18. The Capitol building
19. A shopping center
20. A coal mine

FANTASY THINGS

1. A quart of dried dragon's blood
2. A magic wand
3. A jar containing the north wind
4. Pandora's box
5. Shrinking powder
6. An elf's whiskers
7. King Arthur's sword Excaliber
8. A winged horse
9. A five-hundred pound peach
10. A dictionary of animal language

ACTION WORDS

run	talk
yell	sing
sit	move
fly	work
ride	play

Second-Level Words

swoop	praise
press	create
wrestle	release
swirl	pounce
purchase	seek

IDEAS ABOUT THINGS

thought	fun
hope	law
truth	evil
rule	faith
idea	beauty

Second-Level Words

inspiration	paradise
talent	concept
respect	tyranny
justice	peace
democracy	imagination

FEELINGS TOWARD THINGS

love	fear
sadness	hate
worry	fun
enjoy	excite
anger	surprise

Second-Level Words

pity	sympathy
fury	gratitude
enthusiasm	guilt
ecstasy	terror
loathing	contentment

143

MAKING CREATIVE LISTS

An excellent creative five-minute activity is list making. List making may be followed by story writing, dramatization or elimination and selection activities.

things that make grinding noises
things that flow
blue things (red, green)
greasy things
healthy foods
flitting, flying things
cool, soft things (or warm, hard things)
things that flash
hopeful things
rusty things
things that bounce
happy words
soft words
pretty names
wet things
good smells
sweet things
old things
night sounds
hot-sun things
in-the-sky things
morning things
things lighter than a ball-point pen
sour things
sounds in different places (in a department store, a supermarket, a zoo)
good character traits
people you wish you were like
people outside the class who we like
things you love
things you love to do
mysterious things
things that shine or sparkle
clean things
dreams
things to do on a hot summer day
things to do on a cold rainy day
snowy day things
Christmas things (Halloween, Easter, Valentine)
soft things
things that go boom
illegal things
foreign things
forgotten things
untold things

THINGS TO DO WITH MYSTERY BAGS AND MYSTERY BOXES

Keep a mystery bag and/or mystery box in the classroom. In a five-minute extra time period use one in any of the following ways.

1. Have a treasure hunt for matching things in the bag based only on how they feel in the bag.
2. Describe the object's texture, size, shape.
3. Identify the objects.
4. Identify an object's function.
5. Give a funny function.
6. Tell how each thing relates to a subject or topic being studied (e.g., the American Revolution, another country, living things).
7. Write a story about the thing or things that are felt.
8. Guess the color of the things based only on the way they feel.
9. Have one child tell where the things in the box or bag might be found by feel alone or by looking and having the rest of the class guess what they are.
10. Give clues to the things in the bag or box and have the children guess.
11. Put quotes or directions in the bag or box and draw out a mystery quote or direction each day.
12. Put things in the bag or box suggested by the previous day's events.

OPEN-ENDED SENTENCES

Keep a master file of open-ended sentences. In a five-minute period have children individually finish one or more of the following:

1. The thing I liked best today was _____.
2. If I could be anyone else I _____.
3. Making friends is easy if _____.
4. I like to work when _____.
5. Going home is _____.
6. When I look at my friends and then look at myself I feel _____.
7. The smartest thing I know is _____.
8. When I want to feel happy I _____.
9. If I could have a magic friend I would choose _____.
10. If I could visit someone in another place I would choose _____.
11. Being a friend to a famous person would be fun if _____.
12. The thing I do best is _____.
13. I don't always do what I want to do because _____.
14. The best way to succeed for me is to _____.
15. My favorite meal is _____.

ASSOCIATIONS

Have each child choose a person. Then associate that person with each of the following:

	Friend (Person #1)	Teacher (Person #2)	Person Admired (Person #3)	Person They Live with (Person #4)
a color or a day of the week or a holiday				
three descriptive adjectives				
some particular animal, bird, insect or fish				
a famous person				
a television or movie role they might play well				
an inanimate object				
a musical composition or songs they remind you of				
a different historical event or period they would best fit into				

PERSONAL ASSOCIATIONS

Duplicate for children a list of "times of feeling." Ask them to think of a "theme song" for themselves at each of the times. If this is productive, ask them to think of a motto expressing how they feel, to draw an emblem or flag for themselves at each of these times, or to write a two-line poem.

TIMES OF FEELING FOR CHILDREN

1. When they are *sad*
2. When they are *excited*
3. When they are *frightened*
4. When they are *angry*
5. When they *feel like they are in control*
6. When they feel *adventurous*
7. When they feel *stupid*
8. When they have *really fouled up*
9. When they feel that *people really must like them*
10. When they feel *lonely*

11. When they have *high hopes*
12. When they feel *stubborn*
13. When they feel *wonderful*
14. When they feel *hurt*
15. When they feel *awful*

CUT-UPS

Objective: To develop ability to manipulate materials as a way of solving problems.

Materials: Paper, pencils.

Procedure: Ask children if they can cut a circle into eight pieces (and only eight) using just three cuts. The cuts do not have to be wedge-shaped or straight or equal in size.

Variation: Try other paper cutting problems with children and have them make up their own. (e.g., "Can you fold the paper so as to cut it into five pieces with only one straight cut?") These may also be problems to which answers will not be exact. (e.g., "Can you cut a circle of paper into pieces that can be reformed into a square?")

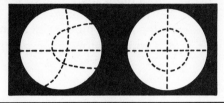

MYSTERY NAME

Objective: To enhance question-asking skills.

Materials: A secret envelope.

Procedure: The teacher selects a student to begin the game. The student chooses a secret person from history, politics, sports, etc. He or she whispers the name of the person to the teacher or writes it on a piece of paper, folds the paper, and puts it into the secret envelope. The class then is invited to ask the student questions about the mystery name. The questions must be phrased to elicit yes or no answers.

The choice of whether or not to use the envelope should be left to the pupil. If it is used it is to be an expression of confidence in his or her ability to be expert about the person selected. The teacher is then permitted to participate in the questions. If it is not used the teacher becomes a helper to the student.

Variations:
1. Have students pose multiple choice questions with the "expert" selecting the correct answer.
2. Use multiple solutions involving associated items from cultures, or historical events studied in class.

Examples: four of the founders of the United States
(Franklin, Jefferson, Washington, Adams)

three of the original thirteen colonies
(Massachusetts, Virginia, New York)

three items associated with George Washington
(wig, monument, Mt. Vernon)

three things a frontier family might eat

three things eaten by an Alaskan Eskimo family

3. The task might have two stages:
   a. to identify the person or place
   b. to identify the items themselves

LAST STRAW

Objective: **To develop decision-making skill.**

Materials: 25 paper or plastic drinking straws.

Procedure: This is a quick game for two people. The object of the game is to force the opponent to pick up the last straw. Each player in turn may pick up one, two, or three straws. Suggest that the children find a way that they can always win.

Variations:
1. Change the object of the game so that the winner is the one who picks up the last straw.
2. Vary the rules so that only one or two straws may be picked up in one turn or not more than four.
3. The student must make a letter with the straws picked up in a single turn. All the letters must spell a single word.
4. Drop the straws and add the rules of Pick-up-Sticks to the existing rules.

☆ SMILE! *asthetic*

Objective: **To encourage thinking about making others happy.**

Materials: Paper, pencil.

Procedure: Tell children to draw a picture in two minutes that will make someone smile. (Note that the smile may be one of amusement or because they are made to feel better.)

Variations:
1. Have children write a single sentence that will make someone smile.
2. Have children *change* a picture on a ditto to make it look happier.

WHAT IS IT?

Objective: **To develop dramatic interpretation skill.**

Procedure: Tell each student to think of an inanimate object to portray. As each person thinks of something, let a student call on another student to become the object. Portrayal may involve movement, body position, and/or facial expression.

Variations:
1. Have a student call on another student to show through imitation, or pantomime a particular sound or smell.
2. Have all students do "mirror" movements during the portrayal.

CAN YOU IMAGINE?

Objective: **To increase power of flexible imagination.**

Materials: Drawing materials for quick sketching and cartooning.

Procedure: Have children think of unlikely and strange images and illustrate them. Examples of things not ordinarily seen are "a dog driving a car," or "a cow on a couch," a "tree in a skyscraper." Things may be unordinary for a number of reasons including the following:

1. They are in unlikely places
2. They have strange features
3. They are an unusual size
4. They are doing unlikely things
5. They are accomplished in an amazing length of time
6. They have strange shapes
7. They have features that are undersized or oversized
8. They have less (or more) features than normal
9. They do things in different ways

Ask students to take a single animal or thing and somehow make it strange in each of these ways.

Variations:
1. Students can be given a list of items with the question, "How many different ways can it be made strange?"
2. Give students incomplete pictures or shapes. Ask them to complete the picture, making it appear strange.
3. Give students pictures of particular scenes. Ask them what could be added to the scene that would be most unusual or what things would they least expect to find in the picture.

SURVEY

Objective: **To develop question-asking skill.**

Materials: Tape recorder.

Procedure: Surveys, and questionnaires are an integral part of modern life. First, make sure that children are familiar with these and the types of questions used. Once they understand the basic process of survey, these activities can be done in a short time. A tape recorder can be used to preserve the discussion and speed it up by eliminating writing. A topic is announced and the children try to make up a five to ten-question survey seeking opinions.

A target survey population may also be announced (e.g., children in the class or in the school, parents, teachers, store owners, project residents).

Some topics to choose from include:
1. Television viewing
2. Attitudes toward tests
3. Reading tastes
4. Favorite foods
5. Attitudes toward elections, government policies, voting.
6. Attitudes toward parents
7. Pet attitudes
8. Ecological habits
9. Favorite hobbies
10. Work attitudes

Variations:
1. Have children make up a "best" test question for a single subject.
2. Have children develop a "fantasy poll" targeted at story characters.

SUPER?

Objective: To develop power to envision criteria of excellence.

Procedure: Have children imagine what particular fantastic powers and sensory abilities could be possessed by various fantasy "super" or wonder characters based on occupation. Encourage humorous descriptions of the following super characters:

1. Carpenter
2. Teacher
3. Lawyer
4. Ant (grasshopper, bee, wasp, spider)
5. Secretary
6. Plumber
7. Assembly line worker
8. Farmer
9. Inventor
10. Sparrow (robin, bluejay, crow)
11. Potato (tomato, carrot)
12. Tree (weed, bush, flower)
13. Veterinarian
14. Animal trainer
15. Janitor

WHAT A MIND

Objective: To develop awareness of the thinking processes.

Procedure: Ask the children to define the word "mind". Guide the discussion so that the children realize that the "mind" is that thing which carries on thought processes. Then ask them to write a definition which is specific to their own individual "mind". Encourage imaginative and unusual definitions. They might include a nickname for their own mind (e.g., "the Fixer," "the Troubled Bubble," the "Marvel Marble").

Variations:
1. Have children draw a picture of the inside of their brain.
2. Have children describe how a thought occurs.

REPEATS

Objective: To increase ability to look for specific details and patterns within a field of numbers or pictures.

Materials: Diagram dittos, various pictures.

Procedure: Begin with a simple square with numbers spread in a haphazard manner. Ask the children to list which numbers are written twice. Then have them look for other repetitions in pictures and diagrams (e.g., figures that are duplicated or nearly duplicated, lines that slant the same way, or colors).

```
3    11    1
              19
18   14   15  18
8         6    1
      9  17   20
2         4    6
```

Variations:
1. Have children look for things that appear only twice and no more.
2. Have children identify only things that are repeated in different ways. (e.g., A number "two" appears alone and as part of a two-digit number. A circle appears as a wheel and as a design in a flag.)

ALPHABET CREATIONS

Objective: **To increase ability to transform.**

Materials: Large letters on paper, and drawing materials.

Procedure: Give each child three or four large letters. Tell them to make them into imaginary numbers or funny characters. Give the new creations names starting with the original letter.

Example:

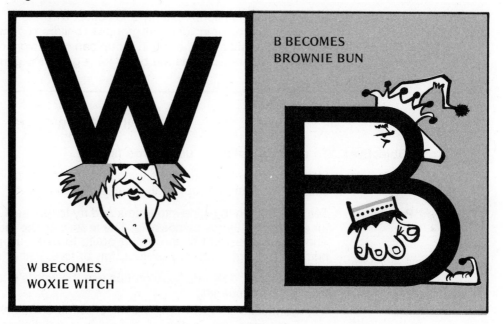

W BECOMES
WOXIE WITCH

B BECOMES
BROWNIE BUN

Variations:
1. Have children create their own brands or signets from the letter.
2. Channel the creativity by characterizing how the letter will be altered. For example, it must be streamlined and made modern, or it must be made old-fashioned, or it must be made to relate to a particular holiday.

THREE WISHES

Objective: **To help clarify goals and values.**

Materials: Paper, pencil.

Procedure: Tell the children to write three wishes. Then have them check to see if the wishes were all for themselves or for someone else. Tell them to write three more wishes; one for themselves, one for another person, and one for everybody in the world. Ask the children if all the wishes are important.

Variations:
1. Limit wishes to either things to have or things to happen.
2. Have the children state three of the wishes in negative form (or positive).
3. Have the children rank the wishes in order of their importance.
4. Relate wishes to a particular holiday or event.

MINI-MYSTERY

Objective: **To develop ability to construct.**

Materials: A series of objects.

Procedure: Tell the children to look at the objects and pick one or several. Have the children create a character or situation around the object(s). Here is a sample list of objects: baseball bat, book, broken pencil, half-eaten apple, handkerchief with some red ink on it.

Variation: Have groups of children identify and collect a series of objects related to a real or storybook person or incident. All groups of children can work with the same characters, traits, or situations, or each group can be assigned a different subject or set. (Their list can be used as the basis for a guessing game.)

MEANINGFUL WORDS

Objective: **To develop ability to use words flexibly.**

Materials: List of words with multiple meanings (for example; point, roll, face, four, sail, hit, set, run, use, mean, rap, seal, steal, sit, ease, tire, try, about, file).

Procedure: Tell the children to divide into teams and try to tell (as a group) as many meanings for each of the words as possible. The team with the most correct meanings wins. The list can be read to the group orally to open up more possibilities through homonyms (e.g., wrap or rap; four, for, or fore; sail or sale).

Variations:
1. Instead of defining, have groups use the words in sentences each showing a different meaning.
2. Conduct a contest with a scoring procedure like basketball, tennis, or hockey. Each team gets a chance to give a new definition or sentence in which the word is used with a different meaning.

STEP UP

Objective: **To develop problem-solving skills.**

Materials: Two sets of large cards. (Each card has one number on it, from zero to nine. If additional children play, numbers must be repeated.)

Procedure: The teacher divides the class into two teams of 10 each. Each student receives a number card. Students are either given an example to compute or an answer for which they must generate a problem. To win a point for their team, they must be the first to step up. For example; they are given the problem: $27 - 3 = $ _____ or $27 - $ _____ $ = 3$. The students holding 2 and 4 must come and stand in the correct order. The first team that "steps up" with the answer shown correctly gets a point. If children are given simply the number 6 they must think of a problem such as 2×3 or $2 + 4$ or $8 - 2$. When a number appears more than once, the child simply moves from one position to the other as the problem is explained. Additional children can be process symbols (for addition, subtraction, multiplication, and division), scorekeepers, or recorders of the problems on the chalk board.

Variations:
1. Use word problems instead of simple computation.
2. Use the number for a date guessing game. (For example, if the year designating the end of World War II were called, children holding 1, 9, 4, and 5, would have to "step up".)

DISAPPEARING WORD

Objective: **To develop absent and missing skills.**

Materials: Blackboard, chalk.

Procedure: The teacher writes a word on the blackboard while the children watch. He/she erases the word as soon as it is written and says, "What word did I send away?"

Variation: This activity can be used also for spelling drills, or for learning homonyms.

TOUCH AND FIND

Objective: **To improve hypothesizing and guessing skills.**

Materials: A bag containing many objects.

Procedure: The teacher passes the bag around as each child draws an object out of it with his eyes closed. When the child figures out what it is, he spells the name of the object.

Variation: Have names of things in the room on slips of paper in the bag. The child must go to the thing he draws and give its name in a sentence.

TOSS THE BALL

Objective: **To develop ability to recognize words and to listen.**

Materials: Cards with words on them, paper clips, ball.

Procedure: The teacher gives each child a card with a word on it and a large paper clip. Then he/she tells the child to clip the word on himself. This word is now his name. The children stand in a circle. One child tosses a ball to someone whose name card he can read. He must call out the word before he tosses the ball. If he should misread the word, the catcher corrects him, states the correct word, and returns the ball to him. The thrower then returns the ball using the correct word. The child whose word has been called becomes the new thrower.

Variations:
1. The caller calls out a sentence. All the children whose words appear in the sentence try to get the ball. (Note: All words in the sentence need not be represented by children.)
2. Assign word duplicates and play playground games in which the two children with the same words compete for the prize ("Steal the Bacon," for example).

MYSTERIOUS SHAPES

Objective: **To help develop skill in identifying shapes.**

Materials: Shoe box, scissors, note cards.

Procedure: Have children cut a circle one-inch in diameter in one end of a shoe box. At the opposite end of the box, cut a circle three-inches in diameter. Cut a three-inch slit in the lid of the box near the larger circle. Give the children cards on which holes have been punched outlining various shapes. Have children place a card in the slit and hold the box up to the light to identify the shape.

Variation: Instead of shapes, use numbers or dots to outline objects.

WORD CHAINS/WORD WEBS

Objective: **To improve verbal expression by developing diverse ways of expressing the same idea.**

Procedure: Use a bulletin board or a drawing on the blackboard to show a chain or a spider's web. Select commonly used words and expressions.

Examples:
verbs–say and said
nouns–dog and cat
adjectives–big and little

adverbs–quickly and slowly
expressions–are you kidding? that's ok

Place a single word or expression at the end of the chain or several at the edges of the web. Build from this lists of other more interesting and synonymous words and expressions. Keep the list(s) visible for several days and add to them. Help children become aware of the way authors convey verbal messages.

Variation: Make chains or webs using antonyms.

THE ALPHABET BALL

Objective: **To develop ability to quickly think of words for specific purposes.**

Materials: A ball.

Procedure: Have children form a circle. The teacher stands in the center and throws the ball to a child saying a letter of the alphabet. The child who catches the ball must respond with a word that begins with that letter. If he misses, he sits down. (Vary this activity by using parts of speech, states, or presidents.)

Variation: The teacher calls a word as the ball is thrown and the child who catches it must use the word in a sentence. (Try synonyms, antonyms, or another word starting with the same letter.)

ADD A LINE

Objective: **To encourage creative conceptualization.**

Materials: Two pencils, two long sheets of paper, two boxes containing the letters of the alphabet each written on a separate slip of paper.

Procedure: Divide class into two teams in parallel rows of desks facing each other. Have the first person on each team draw a letter. He then writes the name of a famous person from American history. The name has to start with the letter drawn from the box (either first or last name). The next person has to write a sentence on the same paper about the person, mentioning some fact about him/her that begins with the same letter. *Example: L*–Abraham Lincoln: he was a lawyer—he was lanky. The first team to finish wins a point.

Variation: Have children create fictional characters instead of real ones.

CHANGE IT

Objective: **To develop a sense of the importance of game rules.**

Materials: Several commercial games.

Procedure: Have children think of a new rule or a rule to be changed in one of the games they normally play. The new or changed rule may make the game more fun to play, easier to play, quicker, more realistic, or simply different. Discuss the many different games that can be played with the same game materials (e.g., playing cards, checkers). Question children about how the differences are manifested.

Variation: Have children design a new playing piece or part for a game.

PROBABILITY

Objective: **To develop understanding of probability.**

Materials: Dittos of sampling sheets and Pick-up-Sticks (several cans).

Procedure: Mix up sticks in several containers so that normal distribution is not true. Have a child shake the container and turn it so only one stick falls through the hole i nthe lid. Record the color of the stick and put a tally mark on the same line in the column labeled sample #1.

COLORS	SAMPLINGS: *(50 draws per sample)*					
	Sample #1		*Sample #2*		*Sample #3*	
	Tally	*Total*	*Tally*	*Total*	*Tally*	*Total*
1						
2						
3						
4						
5						
6						
7						
8						
.						
.						
.						

Return stick to container by putting it through the hole. Then repeat the process. Do this 50 times then total the number of times each color was used. Repeat the activity two more times and record data for each in appropriate columns. Then fill out the following information:

1. I believe there are more _____ sticks than any other color.
2. I believe there are as many _____ sticks as there are _____ sticks.
3. I believe the _____ sticks are fewest in number.
4. My guess for the number of sticks and the odds for drawing one of each color are:

Color	Number	Odds
_____	_____	_____
_____	_____	_____
_____	_____	_____

Variation: Try probability predictions and experiments with dice, coin flips, etc. Then try less predictable kinds of guessing like the number of cars or particular models of cars that will come down a street or go through a particular intersection during a specified time period; or the number of leaves that will fall from a tree in some period of time; or the days it will take for a flower to bloom.

YOUR IMAGINATION

Objective: **To develop ability to project from limited cues.**

Procedure: The teacher draws an irregular shape on the blackboard. Each student uses his imagination and tells what he thinks the object could be.

Variation: Use cards with inkblots, torn paper shapes, or folded paper cutouts.

MIRROR GAME

Objective: **To increase perceptual skills and understanding of the importance of viewing position to the accurate perception of what is seen.**

Materials: Mirror, sample backward words.

Procedure: Tell students to use the mirror to help them identify the code words. Suggest to the children that they write letters or words in a similar code.

Variation: Prepare or have children make designs on a sheet of paper. Then let the children experiment with one mirror and then several standing mirrors set up in various positions. Discuss how the designs are changed, whether or not any combination of mirrors can enable them to see two things simultaneously, and other questions related to mirror image and distortion.

APPLY A QUOTE

Objective: **To develop greater appreciation of the importance of language and expression.**

Materials: Duplicated lists of quotations.

Procedure: The class is divided into teams of four to six children. A leader is appointed and given a list of short quotations (five to fifteen). The list also identifies the authors of the quotes. Teams are given a short period of time to study the list and discuss the original meaning and how all or part of the quote might be applied to a situation today. For example, if the quotation is "I have nothing to offer but blood, toil, tears, and sweat" (Winston Spencer Churchill), the student might apply the last part of this statement to a football game ("Blood, toil, tears, and sweat were the qualities which won Saturday's game").

SAMPLE SITUATIONS

1. Arguments with parents
2. A new friend
3. Going to a party (willingly or unwillingly)
4. Any ball game with a rival
5. Meeting a new person
6. Piano lessons
7. The situation in the Middle East (Ireland, Africa)
8. Gym class (music class, art class)
9. A big test
10. A classmate with a hobby
11. A trip to Walt Disney World

The only thing we have to fear is fear itself.
FRANKLIN DELANO ROOSEVELT

All I know is just what I read in the newspapers.
WILL ROGERS

The truth shall make you free.
JOHN 8:32

You do your worst—and we will do our best.
WINSTON CHURCHILL

Music is well said to be the speech of angels.
THOMAS CARLYLE

We have met the enemy and they are ours.
OLIVER HAZARD PERRY

Be always sure you're right—then go ahead.
DAVY CROCKETT

Where law ends, tyranny begins.
WILLIAM PITT

The earth belongs to the living, not the dead.
THOMAS JEFFERSON

The battle, sir, is not to the strong alone; it is to the vigilant, the active, the brave.
PATRICK HENRY

Character is much easier kept than recovered.
THOMAS PAINE

If you go long enough without a bath, even the fleas will let you alone.
ERNIE PYLE

I do like a bit of butter on my bread.
A.A. MILNE

The most beautiful thing we can experience is the mysterious.
ALBERT EINSTEIN

Nothing happens unless first a dream.
CARL SANDBURG

Variations:
1. Have children write a sentence to precede or follow the quote.
2. Have children select a motto for each day of the week from the quotes.

SOUNDS TELL

Objective: **To develop appreciation for the interdependence of senses.**

Procedure: Have children put on blindfolds and then introduce them to a series of sounds. Let them tell where they would be if they heard these sounds.

Variation: Have children draw a design while blindfolded in accordance with a series of specific directions. Then have them examine their designs against the same design drawn without the blindfold. The designs can be simple or elaborate geometric figures, or combinations of rectangles, stars, circles, circles within circles. The instructions may be given one straight line or curved line at a time or the whole design may be communicated at once.

INVENT AN ADDRESS

Objective: **To increase powers of inventive association.**

Procedure: Famous people and fictional characters should have appropriate addresses. So should people in occupations. Have children make up addresses for various people.

Examples:
the world boxing champ—one, two Punch Street
a fashion model—five N. Style Circle
a famous chef—two T. Recipe Road
a rock singer—Number one Hit Alley

Some people to make up addresses for:

fireman	supermarket cashier
western movie star	automobile manufacturer
television comedian	inventor
secretary	baker
circus strong man	magazine editor
zoo keeper	florist

Variations:
1. Have children create a name for each person's home.
2. Have them create pet names for tools of a trade.

SUBDIVISION

Objective: **To develop categorization skills and ideational fluency.**

Procedure: Give children a simple unlabeled map representing a subdivision or town. Have them label the streets in the subdivision to accord with a particular pattern. They may choose their own pattern or this may be supplied. For example the subdivision might be labeled to emphasize: its beauty (trees, flowers); its heritage (or the national heritage); the world's future; or abstract ideas (faith, hope).

Variations:
1. Have students imagine from the names of the streets what the houses would be like.
2. Have students brainstorm a list of problems the people in the subdivision might have.
3. Have students make up names and addresses for apartments (unrealistically numbered or lettered), or lots in a mobile home park.
4. Have students think of the things the "map" could be.

References

Moore, W. Edgar. *Creative and Critical Thinking*. Boston: Houghton Mifflin, 1969.

Myers, Gary Cleveland. *Highlights Handbook of Creative Thinking Activities*. Highlights for Children, 1965.

Newman, Thelma R. *Creative Candlemaking*. New York: Crown Publishers, 1972.

Osborn, D. Keith, and Dorothy Harpt. *Creative Activities for Young Children*. Detroit, Michigan: Merrell-Palmer Institute, 1964.

Platts, Mary E. *Create*. Education Service Inc., 1966.

Prince, George M. *The Practice of Creativity: A Manual for Dynamic Group Problem Solving*. New York: Harper & Row, 1970.

Raines, Robert A. *Creative Brooding*. New York: Macmillan, 1966.

Raskin, Bernice, comp. *Great Ideas from Learning*. Palo Alto, Ca.: Education Today, 1976.

Rebelsky, Vicky, Roger A. Gooden, and Jeanette Wright. "Creative Arts Program, Description and Evaluation," Unpublished mimeograph by Casady Elementary School. Des Moines, Iowa: (mimeographed) 1971.

Robertson, Malcolm H. *A Method of Stimulating Original Thinking in College Students*. Kalamazoo: Western Michigan University, 1964.

Seuling, Barbara. *Abracadabra: Creating Your Own Magic Show from Beginning to End*. New York: Julian Messner, 1975.

Smith, James A. *Creative Teaching of Reading in the Elementary School*. Boston: Allyn and Bacon, 1975. (Other books in this series each deal with a separate aspect of the curriculum: Language Arts, Music, Art, Science, Social Studies, and Mathematics)

Smith, James. *Setting Conditions for Creative Teaching in the Elementary School*. Boston: Allyn & Bacon, 1966.

Storr, Anthony. *The Dynamics of Creation*. New York: Atheneum, 1972.

Torrance, Ellis Paul. *Rewarding Creative Behavior: Experiments in Classroom Creativity*. Englewood Cliffs, New Jersey: Prentice-Hall, 1965.

Thompson, Richard A. *Energizers for Reading Instruction*. West Nyack, New York: Parker, 1973.

Goldberg, Dorothy K. *The Creative Woman*. Washington: R. B. Luce, 1963.

Wagner, Guy. *Listening Games*. New York: Teachers Publishing Company, Macmillan Company, 1960.

Williams, Frank E. *Classroom Ideas for Encouraging Thinking and Feeling*. Buffalo, New York: D.O.K. Publishers, 1970.

Wooley, A. E. *Creative 35 mm Techniques*. New York: Amphoto, 1970.

Yanes, Samuel and Cia Holdorf. *Big Rock Candy Mountain: Resources for Our Education*. New York: Dell Publishing Co. 1972.

Yoder, Glee. *Take it From There*. Valley Forge, Pa.: Judson Press, 1973.

Young, Milton A. *Buttons Are to Push: Developing Your Child's Creativity*. New York: Pitman, 1970.

Zaratsky, Bill, and Ron Padgett, eds. *The Whole Word Catalogue 2*. New York: McGraw Hill, 1977.

Books with Inspirations for Creative Poetry and Prose Writing and Speech

Barbe, Walter B., ed. *Creative Writing Activities*. Highlights Handbook, published by Highlights for Children, 1965.

Brashers, Howard C. *Creative Writing, Fiction, Drama, Poetry, and the Essay*. New York: American Book Co., 1968.

Carlson, Ruth Kearney. *Sparkling Words: Four Hundred and Twenty-five Practical and Creative Writing Ideas*. Geneva, Illinois: Paladen House Publishers, 1973. (Available through NCTE).

Christensen, Fred. *Springboards to Creative Writing*. Monterey Park California: Creative Teaching Press, Inc., 1971.

Christensen, Fred B. *Recipes for Creative Writing*. Monterey Park, California: Creative Teaching Press, 1966.

Condos, Paulette. *Write On: A Collection of Creative Writing Ideas for Teachers*. Carson, California: Educational Institute, Inc., 1974.

References

Creative Teaching Press. *Story Starters*. Monterey Park, California: Creative Teaching.

Ettner, Kenneth. *A Thousand Topics for Composition*. Urbana, Illinois: NCTE, 1971.

Forte, Imogene, Mary Ann Pangle, and Robbie Tupa. *Cornering Creative Writing*. Nashville: Incentive Publications, 1974.

Gerbranat, Gary L. *An Idea for Acting and Writing Out Language K–12*. Urbana, Illinois: NCTE, 1974.

Glicksburg, Charles Irving. *Creative Writing*. New York: Hendricks House, 1961.

Gunn, M. Agnella, et al. *Creative Approaches to the Teaching of English*. Boston: Boston University School of Education, 1966.

Hillcooks, George, Jr. *Observing and Writing*. Urbana, Illinois: NCTE, 1975.

Hook, Julius N. *Writing Creatively*. Boston: Heath, 1967.

Hopkins, Lee Bennett. *Pass the Poetry Please*. New York: Citation Press, 1972.

Jackson, Jacqueline. *Turn Not Pale, Beloved Snail: A Book About Writing Among Other Things*. Boston: Little Brown and Co., 1974.

Koch, Kenneth. *Wishes, Lies, and Dreams: Teaching Children to Write Poetry*. New York: Random House, 1971.

Landrum, Rogers, and Children from PS 1 and PS 42 in New York City. *A Day Dream I had at Night and other Stories: Teaching Children How to Make Their Own Reader*. New York: Teachers and Writers Collaborating, 1971.

Livingston, Myra Cohn. *When You Are Alone/It Keeps You Capone: An Approach to Creative Writing With Children*. New York: Athenum, 1973.

Mathieu, Aron M. *The Creative Writer: Approach to Creative Writing*. New York: Writer's Digest, 1968.

Mahon, Julia C. *First Book of Creative Writing*. New York: Franklin Watts, Inc., 1968.

Pease, Don. *Creative Writing in the Elementary School*. New York: Exposition Press, 1964.

Pluckrose, Henry. *Creative Themes: A Book of Ideas for Teachers*. London: Evans Brothers, 1969.

St. Onge, Keith R. *Creative Speech*. Belmont, California: Wadsworth Publishing Company, 1964.

Singe, Jerome. *The Child's World of Make Believe*. New York: Academic Press, 1973.

Sklare, Arnold B. *Creative Report Writing*. New York: McGraw-Hill, 1964.

Tiedt, Iris M. *Individualizing Writing in the Elementary Classroom*. Urbana, Illinois: 1975.

Ullyette, Jean M. *Guidelines for Creative Writing*. New York: F.A. Owen Publishing Company, 1963.

Wolfe, Don M. *Creative Ways to Teach English, Grades Seven Through Twelve*. New York: Odyssey Press, 1966.

Sources of Creative Dramatics Ideas

Allstrom, Elizabeth. *Let's Play a Story*. Children's Press, 1957.

Barnfield, Gabriel. *Creative Drama In Schools*. New York: Hart Publishing Company, Inc., 1968.

Burger, Isabel B. *Creative Play Acting: Learning Through Drama*. New York: Ronald Press, 1966.

Chester, Mark, and Robert Fox. *Role-Playing Methods in the Classroom*. Chicago: S.R.A., 1966.

Complo, Sister Juanita Marie. *Drama Kinetics in the Classroom: A Handbook of Creative Dramatics and Improvised Movement*. Boston Plays, Inc., 1974.

Ehreich, Harriet W. *Creative Dramatics Handbook*. Urbana NCTE, 1974.

Goodridge, Janet. *Creative Drama and Improvised Movement for Children*. Boston: Plays, Inc., 1971.

Hoetker, James. *Theater Games: One Way to Drama*. Urbana, Illinois: NCTE, 1975.

Jones, Richard M. *Fantasy and Feeling in Education*. New York: New York University Press, 1968.

Lightwood, Donald. *Creative Drama for Primary Schools*. Glasgow: Blackie, 1970.

References

McCaslin, Nellie. *Creative Dramatics in the Classroom.* New York: David McKay Co., 1968.

McIntryre, Barbara M. *Creative Drama in the Elementary School.* Itasca, Illinois: F. E. Peacock Publishers, Inc., 1974.

Pierini, Mary Paul Francis. *Creative Dramatics: A Guide for Educators.* New York: Herder and Herder, 1971.

Schattner, Regina. *Creative Dramatics for Handicapped Children.* New York: John Day Company, 1967.

Siks, Geraldine Brain, and Hazel Brain Dunnington. *Children's Theater and Creative Dramatics.* University of Washington Press, 1961.

Williams, Frank E. *Classroom Ideas for Encouraging Thinking and Feelings.* Buffalo, New York: D.O.K. Publishers, 1970.

Weissman, Phillip. *Creativity in the Theater.* New York: Basic Books, 1965.

Creative Dance, Music, and Movement Activities Sources

Andrews, Gladys. *Creative Rhythmic Movement for Children.* New Jersey: Prentice-Hall, Inc., 1954.

Carroll, Jean, and Peter Lofthouse. *Creative Dance for Boys.* London: MacDonald and Evans, 1969.

Cherry, Clare. *Creative Movement for the Developing Child.* Palo Alto, California: Fearon Publishers, 1968.

Clemens, James R. *The Music Box.* Inglewood, California: Educational Insights, 1971.

Exiner, Johanna. *Teaching Creative Movement.* Boston: Plays, Inc., 1974.

Fait, Hollis F. *Physical Education for the Elementary School Child.* Philadelphia: W. B. Saunders Co., 1971.

Fleming, Gladys Andrews. *Creative Rhythmic Movement.* Englewood Cliffs, New Jersey: Prentice-Hall, Inc., 1970.

Russell, Joan. *Creative Dance in the Primary School.* London: MacDonald & Evans, Ltd., 1965.

Sheehy, Emma D. *Children Discover Music and Dance.* New York: Teachers College Press, Teachers College, Columbia University, 1968.

Wiener, Jack, and John Lidstone. *Creative Movement for Children, A Dance Program for the Classroom.* New York: Van Nostrand, 1969.

Where to Write for Additional Resource Materials

American Library Association
Children's Service Divison
50 East Huron Street
Chicago, Illinois 60611

Association of Children's Librarians of Northern California
San Francisco Public Library
San Francisco, California

The Child Study Association of America, Inc.
9 East 89th Street
New York, N. Y. 10028

A Cloud Burst of Math Lab Experiment, Vols. I and II
Midwest Publications
P. O. Box 129
Troy, Michigan

Creative Moments Kits
167 Corey Road
Boston, Mass. 02146
(Creative Teaching Press—Story Starters, 1972)

References

Encyclopedia Brittanica Education Corporation
Reference Division
425 North Michigan Avenue
Chicago, Illinois 60611

Fun
Creative Writing by Students, Grades 1–8
P. O. Box 40283
Indianapolis, Indiana 46240

Jack & Jill Magazine
"Poetry by Our Readers"
Saturday Evening Post Co., Inc. Publishers
April, 1974
Number 4, Volume XXXVI

Journal of Creative Behavior
Buffalo, New York: Creative Education Foundation

National Association for the Education of Young Children
1834 Connecticut Avenue, N. W.
Washington, D.C. 20009